Out of the
Black Hole

Out of the
Black Hole

The Patient's Guide
to Vagus Nerve Stimulation
and Depression

CHARLES E. DONOVAN, III

Wellness Publishers, LLC
St. Louis, MO

Published by Wellness Publishers, LLC
www.VagusNerveStimulator.com

Library of Congress Control Number: 2005934797

Donovan, Charles E.
Out of the black hole : the patient's guide to vagus nerve stimulation and depression / Charles E. Donovan. — St. Louis, MO : Wellness Publishers, 2006.

    p. ; cm.
    ISBN 0-9748484-3-3
    ISBN-13: 978-0-9748484-3-3

    1. Donovan, Charles E.—Health. 2. Depressed persons—Care. 3. Depression, Mental—Treatment. 4. Neural stimulation. I. Title.

RC537 .D66 2005
616.85/27—dc22   0411

Printed in the United State of America
10 9 8 7 6 5 4 3 2 1

Editing & Interior design by: Mary Jo Zazueta / www.tothepointsolutions.com
Cover design: Leo Slaninko, Lion's Den, East Brunswick, NJ

*To my family, who never gave up hope,
even when I had lost all hope.*

CONTENTS

FOREWORD

by John Zajecka, MD

The most painful emotions a human being can experience are fear, despair, and hopelessness. These emotions are only among the many symptoms commonly felt by individuals who suffer from major depression.

Over the last several decades, the advances in discovering highly effective treatments, including antidepressant medications, specific psychotherapies, and electroconvulsive therapy have resulted in depression being among the most potentially "treatable" illnesses. Unfortunately, depression remains one of the most prevalent and disabling health problems worldwide.

One of the reasons for the persistence of significant prevalence and disability, despite advances made in treatment, can be attributed to the number of individuals who suffer from "treatment-resistant depression." Among the 19 million individuals with identified depression in the United States alone, over 30 percent are considered treatment-resistant—they either fail to fully respond to multiple treatments (still experiencing significant residual symptoms); fail to show any response to multiple treatments; or initially respond to treatment, but repeatedly lose the response.

This has been a population, similar to those who remain undi-agnosed or inadequately treated, that includes the countless numbers of individuals whose lives are cut short either because of the disabling effects of their depressive symptoms or unnecessar-ily by suicide.

Out of the Black Hole describes the experiences of Mr. Donovan through his journey to find relief from treatment-resist-ant depression. His description exemplifies the experience faced by those who suffer from depression, as well as family, significant others, and health care providers who are along the same journey. Through his perseverance and commitment to relief, Mr. Donovan describes his recovery with vagus nerve stimulation (VNS), a recently FDA-approved treatment for treatment-resist-ant depression—providing a testimony of hope for those who still suffer.

As a psychiatrist who has dedicated a career of nearly twenty years toward improving our understanding and management of treatment-resistant depression, I am honored to have the oppor-tunity to convey my personal enthusiasm and message of hope, as conveyed by Mr. Donovan, for the role that VNS may provide for both individuals who suffer from treatment-resistant depression and for their health-care providers.

When I was first approached to be an investigator for VNS for treatment-resistant depression as a Chicago-area site, in the study which Mr. Donovan participated in St. Louis, I felt excited for the opportunity to use a potentially effective treatment for the many depressed patients who were resistant to conventional treatments. I also reacted with a degree of caution, not wanting to become overly confident until the "real data" proved to be effective, toler-ated, and safe.

While I was aware of the FDA-approval of VNS for treatment (medication)-resistant epilepsy for many years, another initial reaction was my concern about how my patients may accept a treatment that required surgery, even though I knew it was minimally invasive.

As the study progressed, my enthusiasm grew stronger. My concerns about efficacy, safety, tolerability, and acceptance/willingness of this patient population to have this procedure were replaced with confidence in what I experienced with many of the patients whose lives (including those of their families) were consumed with a chronic illness and then gradually transformed to relief of symptomatic suffering and returned to a level of functioning that was no longer dictated by their depression.

As described by Mr. Donovan's experience, the patients who improved typically showed a gradual improvement. While some showed modest improvement within the first twelve to sixteen weeks, I was most impressed with the continued improvement over time and that many went on to full remission. These observations, combined with my seeing the same patients who in the past lose a response over time, sustain responses now beyond two years, have convinced me of the sustained efficacy in many people who had failed to respond and/or sustain the response to aggressive treatments in the past.

As time passed, I realized my own experience paralleled that of the other sites that took part in the study, and a similar group of treatment-resistant patients who did not receive VNS showed less response than those who received treatment.

I learned in medical school that the vagus nerve plays an important role in the regulation of many physiological functions, including a role in the regulation of mood and emotional stability. The story finally began to come together, two decades later, as the clinical data emerged from this landmark study for treatment-resistant depression—that stimulation of the vagus nerve regulates areas of the brain and neurotransmitters in the brain hypothesized to play a role in the regulation of mood, including the symptoms of major depression.

From this innovative treatment for depression, we have learned more about the possible mechanism(s), and provide a model to develop treatments even beyond VNS.

As with any illness, and any treatment, there have been those who do not show a significant response. For some, they have shown improvement with time. The majority of patients in this study elected to continue their treatment, realizing we are learning more each day about ways to optimize the best outcomes.

I feel fortunate to have been part of the pivotal trial that resulted in this landmark FDA-approval of VNS for treatment-resistant depression, and receiving approval for the same indication in both Canada and Europe, prior to the United States FDA-approval. I commend those who remained committed to carry out the studies, and advocates to support a treatment for treatment-resistant depression. The real heroes are the patients who took part in the trials.

As a clinician, there is no better feeling than to be part of the process of relieving the suffering of depression, and to observe the actual return of enjoying life, feeling passion. Mr. Donovan provides an accurate account of his recovery through VNS. *Out of the Black Hole* conveys hope to those who continue to search for relief of their depression, and for those who are at their side, either as family, friends, significant others, those providing spiritual guidance, those in the workplace, as well as those of us who are the health-care providers. . . . never give up.

Mr. Donovan's personal testimony provides hope and perseverance to overcome the fear and despair of depression.

O

FOREWORD

by Nancy Williger, PhD

The devastating effects of long-term, chronic depression can barely be imagined by those who are exempt from its grip and can barely be described by those who suffer in its shadow. In the thirty years of my practice in psychology and social work, too many times I have watched lives being consumed by the illness. The added layer of shame for suffering from an illness that is not seen as quite "legitimate" by friends and relatives, makes it even more difficult. Isolation is often the only alternative when it feels so hard to be with others and feel so alone. Worse yet, those who love someone who is depressed, often say "just buck up" and "you can get over it" in an effort to cheer them up.

It has been a joy to watch the transformation of Mr. Donovan as he has emerged from his depression of many years. When I met him, he was completely isolated and woke every day emotionally paralyzed by his illness. Now he has moved from his extreme self-focus to seeing friends and family, and finally to writing this book as a way to help others. He has achieved a sense of perspective about his life that is demonstrated by his dry sense of humor.

As a therapist, I often learn as much from my patients as I hope they learn from me. Working with Mr. Donovan has been one of those experiences. I believe I have never met anyone more committed to his recovery. He was willing to do anything to feel better, including becoming a participant in the vagus nerve study. In this book, he describes the descent into his illness with humor and pathos. Then he goes on to describe the surgery that led to his recovery. His willingness to rise above his own shame about his suffering so that others can learn about a new and exciting treatment is admirable. This book is a must read for anyone, whether layperson or professional, who is seeking hope for the treatment of depression.

NANCY WILLIGER, PHD

ACKNOWLEDGMENTS

The author gratefully acknowledges the following individuals and organizations:

Richard Bucholz, MD; Charles Conway, MD; Marc Deschamps; Werner Doyle, MD, Eduardo Garcia-Ferrer, MD; Misha Getter; JoAnn Filla-Taylor, RN; Linda Greensfelder, PhD; Rachel Feinberg, MD; Hara Estroff Murano; Ed Rivera, PA; Anthony F. Sansone, Jr. and family; Roxann Schroeder, PhD; Leo and Diane Slaninko; Raymond Tait, PhD; Amanda Tennant, MSPT; Tony Vitale, CPT; Nancy Williger, PhD; Nickie Wrenn; Mary Jo Zazueta; Tanya Zimmerli; Medscape.com; New York University Medical Center; Patient Advocate Foundation; *Psychology Today Magazine*; St. Louis University Hospital; and Walsworth Publishing Company.

And a special thank you to each and every one of the 500 employees at Cyberonics, who tirelessly researched and developed this extraordinary life-saving, life-altering medical device.

O

INTRODUCTION

Everybody has a story. My story is the one I know best and can write about. It is not a memoir of chemical dependency or self-abuse. Those subjects have been written about many times. This is a story of my winning battle against depression and the vagus nerve stimulation treatment that saved my life by bringing me *Out of the Black Hole*. And, this is the first book to be published about winning the battle with a medical implant procedure called VNS Therapy™.

On July 15, 2005, the U.S. Food and Drug Administration (FDA) approved vagus nerve stimulation "for the adjunctive long-term treatment of chronic or recurrent depression for patients 18 years of age or older who are experiencing a major depressive episode and have not had an adequate response to four or more adequate antidepressant treatments." Cyberonics, the manufacturer of the VNS Therapy System™ is in the process of educating psychiatrists nationwide about the first ever FDA-approved informatively labeled, long-term treatment option for the lifelong and life-threatening illness of depression.

Personally, I don't believe the stigma associated with depression has changed one bit in the past century, so I was apprehensive about sharing my story. After all, I had spent the majority of my life hiding my depression from family, friends, and business associates—and now I was writing a tell-all book.

I wrote the main part of this book as if I were having a conversation with a close friend who was looking for guidance with his or her debilitating chronic depression. I discuss the misery I experienced, the seemingly unending search for answers, the vagus nerve implant procedure itself, and my subsequent recovery from the grip of depression.

The second half of the book includes a description of the ninety-minute, outpatient implant procedure, detailed information and pictures of the VNS Therapy System™, and things to consider while deciding to have the procedure. Also included are the insurance codes, the insurance reimbursement process and the latest information about the disease of depression from the American Psychiatric Association.

I also wrote *Out of the Black Hole: The Patient's Guide to Vagus Nerve Stimulation and Depression* for the loved ones of people who suffer from depression. When a patient reaches the severe, chronic level of this disease, often it is their family members who are making the medical decisions. At the other extreme, the family members may be in the dark about what is going on between the doctor and the patient, or they don't trust the information that they're receiving from their loved ones. One thing is for certain, the lack of knowledge about this disease and not knowing the best way to help and interact with the suffering loved one complicates everything.

I have been fortunate throughout my life because I have always had access to the best medical care available (for any illness), and I have a close and supportive family. I don't know how people survive severe depression if they don't have access to good doctors, the latest pharmaceutical drugs, psychologists, psychiatrists, and a strong support group. Many depressed patients have none of the above, yet they still endure. Their stories, in many ways, are more remarkable than mine. Senator Hillary Rodham Clinton wrote a book titled *It Takes a Village*. It's about how we can shape our society into the kind of village that enables children to grow into able, caring, resilient adults; physically, intellectually, emotionally, and spiritually. If my family wrote a similar book about the past ten years of my life, it would be titled *It Took Heaven, Earth and VNS Therapy*™ So, I've also written this book for them.

Let's get started.

Out of the
Black Hole

O

chapter one

THE STIGMA OF DEPRESSION

Have you ever watched a television show where a famous celebrity dispenses the advice: "Just take your antidepressants and you'll get better?" I have, and it really makes me mad. For instance, one night I was watching the *Larry King Show* on CNN and Mike Wallace was the guest. Mr. Wallace has courageously and bravely talked publicly about his long struggle with depression. I applaud him for that. It took a lot of guts.

On this particular night, at the end of the show, Mr. Wallace pointed to the camera and said, "Take the antidepressants prescribed by your doctor, because they work." But he left out two critical words: "for him." They work for him. And he is damn lucky that the antidepressants work. It's pure luck of the draw whether or not antidepressants work for a depressed person. It's not a character flaw or due to a person's laziness; it's simply that the chemical balances oftentimes don't work.

Imagine walking through the borough of Manhattan, population 1.2 million people. It's crowded. The number of people nationwide who are not helped by antidepressants is FOUR times greater. At least 4.8 million Americans suffer from chronic or treatment-resistant depression. None of the available antidepressants work for them. I doubt that Mr. Wallace has to check with the human resource's department at CBS to see how many mental health office visits he is allowed each year or what his co-payments are for a brand-name antidepressant. (I am not picking on Mr. Wallace; he is a skilled reporter and an early supporter of mental health issues. I admire him for being the first major celebrity to bring his depression out of the closet and share it with the public.)

I am also saddened when I hear the commercial for the *Oprah Winfrey Show* that has a voice-over of an audience member saying "you inspire me to live the best life that I can" followed by Oprah's voice-over of "every moment is worth celebrating." I can't think of anyone who has accomplished more things and motivated more people than Oprah Winfrey. However, many people who suffer from treatment-resistant depression (TRD) are biologically unable to celebrate life. It's impossible. You can't be talked out of any biological disease. When a TRD patient hears messages like this, it only makes him feel worse. I am not suggesting that Oprah change her commercial, but I do have tremendous respect and sensitivity for people who suffer from chronic depression. I have walked a mile in their shoes.

Chronic depression is a biological illness, just like cardiovascular disease and cancer. Depression is not in your head; it is in your brain. Depression is now recognized as a neurodegenerative disorder. Prolonged depression may result in progressive and cumulative damage to the brain. *Psychology Today Magazine* summarized the latest findings about depression, as presented at the American Psychiatric Association's annual meeting in May 2004 (see Appendix D).

Educate yourself and your family about this disease. You can eliminate a lot of the frustration and confusion about this baffling disease by keeping up-to-date on the latest scientific information.

Many sufferers of depression do not seek help because of the stigma associated with mental illness. Sometimes family and friends contribute to this image when they continually urge a depressed person to "snap out of it" or "get on with your life" or "count your blessings." I know the person means well; but it's time to blow that type of advice out of the water. It doesn't work. In fact, it makes a person feel more ashamed and more depressed.

If things get bad enough, some people become suicidal. Almost 500,000 suicide attempts each year are serious enough to warrant a trip to the emergency room. Suicide is the eighth leading cause of death in the United States, but it is virtually 100 percent preventable with treatment from a mental health caregiver (psychiatrist, psychologist, social worker). Unfortunately, there is a successful suicide attempt every forty-five minutes, twenty-four hours a day, seven days a week. Although women are more predisposed to depression than men, four times more men actually commit suicide. Personally, I think the suicide statistics and the number of people suffering from chronic depression are under-reported.

O

chapter two

Into the Black Hole

Although this chapter is at the beginning of the book, it was one of the last chapters I actually wrote. Much to the chagrin of my editor, the thought of writing about my personal experience with depression was the greatest source of procrastination for me. I dreaded it. I didn't know what to say. It felt too invasive.

For insight on how to get started, I read the memoirs of people who suffered from depression. It only made things harder. While I found many self-help books on the subject of depression, I couldn't find any firsthand stories of lengthy battles with chronic depression. There were many different stories, but none that I could relate to.

There were stories written by people with manic and bipolar depression. Some of these people would book a first-class airline ticket to France on a moment's notice, gamble a hundred thousand dollars in Monte Carlo, have sex with all sorts of creatures, drop fifty thousand dollars on a shopping spree in Paris, return to the States, and then crash after having been awake for seventy-two hours straight. I couldn't believe what I was reading. It was incredible, but it wasn't me.

There were a few books even more dramatic and serious, about people with histories of multiple suicide attempts, paranoid schizophrenia, and numerous personality disorders. Once again, these weren't in any way related to my experience with depression.

I worried that readers would be bored to death by the simplicity of my life, a garden-variety patient suffering from severe chronic depression. Or even worse, I feared my depression was some sort of bizarre or abnormal illness. It's one thing to have depression, but it's another thing to have had weird depression. I needed a catalyst to get this chapter going. So, recently, during the last two minutes of an appointment with my psychologist, I sheepishly squeezed in a quick question: "I just want to make sure that what I told you about the way I felt and what I did, do you hear that type of stuff from other patients?"

She nodded and said, "Yes, I hear the same exact information from many of my patients suffering from depression."

I was relieved. I'm normal—whatever that means. Having been inspired by the doctor's answer, I decided it was time to finally start this chapter and get it over with. However, the main purpose of this book is to educate people about vagus nerve stimulation therapy for depression. It's not going to be a long, detailed journey about my battle with depression. That's far too dull. But I think some of this information is necessary to clarify why I qualified for inclusion in the investigational study.

I am going to speed through the first forty years of my life. They are important, but the past five years are much more significant to this book.

There is a history of depression on both sides of my family. As in most families, it wasn't talked about. Within my immediate family, I got the gene. On December 9, 1968, when I was eleven, my mother tragically died in a house fire.

In 1968, medical wisdom said children didn't get depressed. Ironically, I kept hearing this over and over: "Children are resilient, they bounce back quickly." The reality, however, was that I was completely devastated by my mother's death. I never got the chance to say good-bye. I never had the chance to tell her how much I loved her one last time. I am still haunted by that night.

Whenever I see a videotape of Prince William and Prince Harry walking behind their mother's casket, somberly staring at their feet, I am reminded of walking by my mother's casket at her funeral, unable to even glance up as her body was ushered out of the church.

Today we know children do get depressed; I guess I was just ahead of my time. We also know that most depressive episodes are preceded by a stressful event. I have never discussed this with my father, but in the summer of 1969 I was sent off to camp. My other three siblings (all younger) were not. I can only assume I was not bouncing back quickly.

In another strange twist, my roommate at the camp committed suicide in 2002. I had known him for thirty-three years.

My father remarried a year after my mother died and two families were merged together. Three girls and three boys; we were like *The Brady Bunch* gone crazy.

I did not appear to have depression in my teen years. However, in retrospect, it's clear I was suffering from depression. I know I didn't handle stress as well as my siblings did.

It's not that they didn't have their own issues to deal with, but they led normal lives. For me, this was the beginning of isolation, tension, and anxiety. I spent most of my time in my bedroom with the door closed.

I could not understand why I was so stressed out as a child. My brothers and sisters did not feel the same levels of anxiety that I did. Now, I know why: depression. Children, teenagers, and adults with depression do not react the same way to external events as normal people do. Depressed people (including children) have a much more exaggerated reaction to what is going on around them. We take things more personally and seriously.

Researchers have now recognized that the loss of a parent in childhood is associated with adult psychiatric disorders, including depression, anxiety, and posttraumatic symptoms. Apart from heredity and recent stress, childhood trauma is the most common predictor of major depression in adults. Childhood trauma and loss can cause prolonged hypersensitivity to stress by upsetting the regulation of the sympathetic nervous system.[*]

---

[*] *Harvard Mental Health Letter,* June 2005.

O

chapter three

THE 1980s

In the spring of 1980 I was a senior at Georgetown
University. After the demise of a close friendship, I had a major
depressive episode that lasted for months. I couldn't concentrate,
I couldn't pay attention during my classes, and I couldn't study. I
feared I would flunk out the second semester of my senior year.
Up until that point I had a solid B+ average. But I couldn't do the
work anymore. I had little short-term memory. My new motto
was "D for diploma."

Finally, out of desperation, I made an appointment with a psychologist at the student health center. I had accepted a job in New
York City in the management training program of what is now
J.P. Morgan Chase. The only thing I remember about the
appointment is that the psychologist told me to get into therapy
as soon as I arrived in New York.

In the summer of 1980, I moved to New York. I found a psychologist by going through the yellow pages. In New York,
everything is location, location, location. I lived at 141 East 55th
Street, Apt. 5A. I chose a psychologist who had his practice in the

same building, Apt. 7N. There was so much shame and stigma of being in psychotherapy that I didn't even tell my roommate I was seeing a psychologist. After my 6:00 p.m. appointment I would walk from the psychologist's office, down two floors to my apartment, and tell my roommate that I was just getting home from work.

That was the beginning of learning how to hide my depression. (It's a skill that people with depression are very good at it.)

After a year with my psychologist "in residence" I switched to a high-profile Park Avenue psychiatrist. He was a published author, had been quoted in *Newsweek* and *Time* magazines, and had been a guest on the *Phil Donahue Show*. At the time, I thought this meant something. It didn't. Of note is that in 1981 a high-profile Park Avenue psychiatrist charged $125 per session compared to $35 per hour for the psychologist in my building. I didn't get my money's worth.

Enough gloom and doom for the moment.

I had a great time in New York in the 1980s. It was an incredibly fun experience. I stayed out late most nights, went to many parties, danced to Lester Lanin and his Orchestra at the Pierre Hotel, dined at Le Cirque, and partied at the Mud Club until closing time. I was a frequent flyer at Studio 54, the Tunnel, the Limelight (before it became tacky), Danceteria, the Palladium, the Surf Club, and Doubles. There were limousine rides to Bruce Springsteen concerts, first-class airline travel, dinner and dancing at The Rainbow Room, countless fourth-row orchestra seats at Broadway shows, a house at the beach every summer, blah, blah, blah.

Living in New York in my twenties was exciting and exhilarating; but it was also a lot of stress on a consistent basis. It never let up.

Stress is not good for people with depression. Fortunately I was able to grind through the stress and depression and have some fun. I was driven to succeed. I read somewhere that you should thrive at your job as opposed to strive. I was striving. There's a subtle difference. It's significantly more work for your mind and body if you are not thriving at work. My depression was manageable and I worked hard not to let things discourage me or get me down. But the depression was always there, lurking in the background.

I drank a lot of alcohol and swallowed many prescription pills. After less than two months in New York (at the age of twenty-one) I did not feel well, so I made an appointment with a medical doctor a few blocks up the street from where I lived (location, location, location). He was a Harvard Medical School graduate in his mid-seventies. I climbed the steps to his office on the second floor of a walk-up office building. I thought it was a little odd to have an office in a walk-up building. But this was New York City and it was not unusual at all. He gave me a prescription for 2-milligram Valium tablets, which was the lowest available dosage. I had never heard of Valium before, but for me, it turned into "the pause that refreshes." Valium relaxed me. All of a sudden things didn't seem so bad. Valium lowered my anxiety level. I felt better. The "pain" went away. So, I just kept getting the prescription refilled.

The following year my physician retired, so I went to another doctor, who upped the dosage to 5-milligram tablets. Then I discovered that if I mixed Valium with alcohol I got a better bang for my buck.

Many times I was a nervous wreck at the office. Working on Wall Street is stressful, and if you have depression, you can multiply the stress two- or three-fold. So the doctor upped my dosage to 10-milligram tablets of Valium. My drinking became heavier and my requests for Valium refills were more frequent. Incredibly, I was convinced I had absolutely no drug or alcohol problem.

In 1989 I moved back to my hometown of St. Louis. By then,

my drinking had gotten completely out of control, yet still, nobody knew about it. I often drank by myself. Valium was practical because it didn't smell, I could easily carry it with me wherever I went, and, best of all, it had no calories! Many times I took 50 milligrams of Valium throughout the day and then drank three-fourths of a bottle of Wild Turkey or Stoli in the evening and passed out on the couch in my family room. What was I thinking? How could I be so stupid? (And this is a cleaned-up version.)

Thanksgiving 1989. I was in my twentieth day at the Hyland Center, a drug and alcohol treatment facility in St. Louis. Three weeks earlier I told my boss where I was going. He actually thought I was taking a 28-day vacation. Sadly, ignorance about the disease of alcoholism hasn't changed much in fifteen years.

One of my closest friends from seventh grade died of complications from alcoholism in March 2003. I found his body. I didn't know he had a drinking problem until just a few weeks before he died. He was great at hiding and deception and I was really stupid. I, along with his closest friends, had planned an intervention, which ironically was scheduled the day of his funeral. Too little, too late.

Alcoholism and depression often go hand in hand; they now call it "dual diagnosis." I certainly had both. This was back in the heyday of treatment centers. The Hyland Center had a wonderful treatment program. The staff was expertly trained in substance abuse, psychological and mental health problems, and how to help patients recover from their addictions. I was fortunate to have this type of treatment center available to me. I never could have recovered on my own. I was a falling-down drunk and nobody saw it. I know alcoholics are good at hiding and deceiving, but I think people who suffer from depression are even better at hiding their disease, especially since depression doesn't smell like a Wild Turkey Manhattan straight up!

It should be noted that the majority of substance abuse centers have been closed because insurance companies won't pay for residential treatment. Some insurance firms will pay for outpatient treatment, which is mostly worthless. Basically the alcoholic goes to a facility in the morning for a few hours of lectures and then returns home early in the afternoon in time for cocktail hour. It's crazy.

When I first walked into my home on December 4, 1989, after my stay at the Hyland Center, a small artificial Christmas tree was waiting for me on the family room coffee table. A signed card, dated 12-4-89, read: "With Love, Mom and Dad." Christmas 2004 will be the fifteenth time I've used the tree to celebrate my recovery and remind me of my family's continuous love.

My first day back at work (after being away for a month), I was nervous and ashamed. I had a private office less than fifteen feet from the elevators. My plan was to get off the elevator and head straight to my office, unseen. The elevator arrived on the seventh floor and the doors opened. I took three or four steps and then I heard shouting from the other side of the room. "Hey, Charlie's back. Charlie Donovan is back!" Oh brother, my plan hadn't worked.

This miniature Christmas tree greeted Charlie on December 4, 1989, upon his return from rehabilitation at the Hyland Center. He still uses the tree each holiday season as a reminder of his sobriety.

O

chapter four

THE 1990S

My depressive episodes gradually became more frequent, severe, and protracted in duration; and it took longer for me to recover from them—until finally I never did recover. This is not an unusual pattern for people suffering from treatment-resistant depression. The depression gets worse and more frequent over the years. I was depressed all the time. Unfortunately, there were no spontaneous expensive trips to Paris, I stayed in one place: the mental health gutter.

In the early 1990s, life was fine. I was completely sober, I earned a good income, and had some fun. But by 1995, I had serious financial setbacks, job turmoil (having nothing to do with my performance), and I was under more stress than I had ever been.

I couldn't eat, couldn't sleep, and woke up every morning at 5:00 a.m., scared to death, with my heart racing in my chest. This anxiety lasted all day, every day. Week after week. Month after month. I would go to work and put on a happy face, but my career was being ruined by the lies and decision making of the senior management of the Wall Street firm I worked for. I foolishly (my fault) kept hoping that management would deliver on their promises to me, but they never did.

Financially, I was taking a beating. The assault on my mind and body from the nonstop stress was brutal. I never got a break, not even for a minute.

In the fall of 1995, the firm that I worked for was named the lead underwriter on a new bond offering. I worked diligently to sell this thing when the offering went public (to large institutional investors). I hustled.

The day came for the deal, November 20, 1995. NAC Re Corporation issued $100,000,000 of 7.15 percent notes due November 15, 2005. I sold more of the offering than any other salesman nationwide, resulting in a net commission to me of $50,000. I was relieved at the end of that long day. But I was not happy.

I must have collapsed or my behavior became alarmingly irrational, because that night my parents hospitalized me. I have no recollection of what happened. I don't even remember being driven to the hospital or being admitted. I had never been a believer in repressed or blocked memories, but I am now.

I remember waking up at 7:30 the next morning. I was lying on a narrow hospital bed, staring at the ceiling, asking myself, "How am I ever going to get my life back?" Then I picked up my cell phone and called my boss. In my cheeriest voice, I said "Hi Richard, it's Charlie."

"Hi Chaz," he said. "You had an unbelievable commission day yesterday; the whole office is talking about it. Great job!"

"Thank you very much," I said. "I appreciate it. But I am feeling a little under the weather today. I won't be coming into the office."

I returned to work about a week later.

I don't know how in the world my cell phone came with me to the hospital. Nine years later, I still don't carry a cell phone on a regular basis. However, that morning it was a good thing I had it with me. Let me gracefully say that I was in a department of the hospital that didn't provide phones with cords in the patients' rooms.

My thinking became more irrational, exaggerated, and unproductive.

We know now that the depressed brain is different than a normal person's brain. The hypothalamus of people with depression tends to be reduced in size, and this can exaggerate normal moods. Consequently, depressed people respond more vigorously to threats from their external environment. Half of all major depressive episodes are preceded by a stress event. This stress event was precipitated by the destruction of my career and financial problems. Things continued to unravel quickly. However, I would never be able to make a rationale, informed decision about my career or find happiness until I could get the albatross of depression off my back. Or more accurately, out of my brain.

From 1994 to 1999, I changed jobs five times. More stress, more anxiety, increased severity of depression. I was searching for happiness and could not find it. In 1998 I accepted a job at a bank with a 90 percent pay cut. I couldn't believe how poorly the employees were treated. I'm not looking for pity, but it was a tough bullet to bite. The shame and stress brought on another major bout of depression.

Although I owned my own home, I had to move back into my parents' house because I needed their unconditional love and support. I never would have survived without them.

Each morning I'd wake up with my heart pounding and my whole body aching. I'd put on a suit, pump myself up, go to work, and fake contentment all day long. I don't know how I did it. And, eventually, I couldn't do it.

My family had no idea what to do. (No family does.) They were worried, confused, and frustrated. One Saturday morning, as my mom opened the door to the patio for me, she said, "It's a beautiful day. Go take a walk in the park. Just go! Right now!" (If I had a nickel every time someone told me to take a walk in the sunshine because it would make me feel better, I'd be a millionaire.) So, I went for a walk in the park. It was a nice spring day, but I couldn't appreciate the beauty of the blooming dogwood trees or the gorgeous color of the budding azaleas. I couldn't smell the fresh sweetness of the spring air. I was unable to experience any joy or pleasure. I only felt pain, misery, and emptiness. The dichotomy between the beautiful day and how I felt on the inside only made me feel worse.

About fifteen minutes later, my mom drove to the park to find me. "Get in the car," she said. "Your psychiatrist wants to see you. Now!" Apparently as soon as I'd left for the park, Mom placed a desperate call to his office. She pleaded with him and said there must be something more that he could do to help her son. She couldn't believe there was *nothing* left to try. Realize at this point, I had been on every possible combination of antidepressants and antipsychotic medications available. And I was still religiously taking all the medications that he had prescribed, but they were not working.

My parents drove me to the psychiatrist's office. They were full of hope but I had low expectations. My psychiatrist had run out of bullets, and I knew it. I didn't know what more he could say, but at least he could validate that I had tried all the available medications. People lose credibility when they have depression, so I was glad my parents would hear the information directly from the psychiatrist. I know sometimes they didn't believe I was doing all that I could.

This is a partial list of the medications that had been prescribed for me over the years. None of them gave me long-term relief. They are in no particular order.

Imipramine	Lithium	Remeron
Prozac	Effexor	Provigil
Serzone	Wellbutrin	Trazodone
Nortriptyline	Zyprexa	Risperdal
Zoloft	Elavil	Paxil

A nurse ushered us into the doctor's office. We talked for about ten minutes, and then he said, "Well, there is one more thing we could try." My parents and I moved to the edge of our seats. What was it? Then he dropped a bombshell: shock treatments. There was a minute of silence before he explained the procedure carefully and thoroughly. I said okay to a series of electroconvulsive treatments (ECT). There was no negotiation necessary. I was willing to try anything. I made the appointment for the first treatment and then we left his office.

I do remember how happy Mom and Dad were. They were both smiling. They were excited that I was going to try a new type of treatment. I think this gave them hope that there was still another potential solution available, a cure for this incurable disease. I, however, burst into tears. I was a thirty-nine-year-old man sobbing like a baby and hugging my parents. I had never cried in front of my parents before.

Shock treatments! I couldn't believe it. You can't sink any lower on the depression treatment spectrum than shock treatment. And I had hit it.

Later that same Saturday, I went to a black-tie fund-raising dinner at the Ritz-Carlton. It was an event I had committed to months ahead of time that I couldn't get out of. Incredibly, I floated, seemingly effortlessly, from table to table, smiling and laughing at all the right times. As far as anyone knew, I had spent the day relaxing on the golf course. I look back now and wonder how I pulled it off. This was an extreme example, but I had "pulled it off" hundreds of times over the years.

O

chapter five

WHAT, NO CASSEROLES?

Nobody brings you a casserole when you're having shock treatments. I read that somewhere and thought it was hilarious. And it's true. I didn't tell anyone I was having shock treatments and I don't think my family did either. It was a tightly guarded secret. Don't ask, don't tell, and don't want to know.

My memory surrounding the period in which I received ECT is fragmented. It was the summer of 1998. I was still staying at my parents' home. My dad would drive me to the hospital at 7:00 in the morning, and I was home by 11:00 a.m.

I think I had a series of fifteen treatments. Midway through the series of ECT treatments my family changed psychiatrists. I don't remember a thing about this. All I can say is that my family took me to the best psychiatrist in St. Louis. His endless patience, incredible compassion, and tremendous insight into the disease of depression saved me. The comfort I felt at his unfailing kindness during every session motivated me to work through the pain, stay hopeful, and maintain the will to survive. His knowledge of psycho-pharmaceuticals was always on the cutting edge. I still see him for medication management visits. He keeps me in balance. His low-key, low-pressure approach helped offset the high pressure I was under to "snap out of it." I will never be able to repay him for his kindness.

I took a short medical leave of absence during the last half of the ECT treatments. Apparently in the beginning there were some days when I would have a shock treatment in the morning and return to work in the afternoon. I had a lot of pressure from my family to return to work as soon as possible. Their yardstick for my improvement was my putting on a suit and tie and going to work. They strongly felt that it was not a good idea to sit around the house and do nothing.

The mention of shock treatments (ECT) brings up comparisons with Jack Nicholson's role in the 1979 movie *One Flew Over The Cuckoo's Nest*. Unlike the shock treatments, I would be much more open about telling close friends about my vagus nerve stimulator implant procedure. For whatever reason, I didn't feel anything close to the stigma that was associated with ECT. The physical solution (implant procedure) to a mental health problem carried less of a stigma than electric shocks.

So I returned to work, but much too soon. My first day back I didn't know what day of the week it was or even which floor I worked on. Was it the sixteenth or the seventeenth? I couldn't remember. I was terribly self-conscious and uncomfortable returning to work after an unexplained three-week absence. I am sure it was bizarre for my co-workers. Something happened, but what? This was another one of those "don't ask, don't tell, don't want to know" situations. I was crushed by the shame and embarrassment of the shock treatments. The cover-up was on in full force.

I made it to my desk, but I couldn't remember how to turn on the computer—let alone how to use it. I sat there for about an hour, shuffling papers from one side of the desk to the other, trying to think of a plan. I was good at masquerading, but I quickly decided I couldn't perform miracles. I knew I had to come clean with someone, because this memory loss wasn't going to improve in one day. Fortunately there was a wonderful woman in the next cubicle named Denise. Denise was and is a saint. I went into her cubicle and quietly explained I needed her help. She never asked one personal question. She took me by the hand, walked into my cubicle, pulled up a chair, and started from square one, saving me from any further embarrassment in the office. Her empathy and genuine kindness were truly extraordinary. She freely gave of her time to get me jump-started. In any event, within a few weeks 80 percent of my memory returned, the other 20 percent never came back.

I don't regret for a minute my decision to have ECT. In fact, there was no doubt I'd do it since there was nothing else left to try. But it didn't work for me. A year or so later my family told me that I looked absolutely horrible during this period.

As my depression worsened in 1998 and 1999, it became harder and harder to learn new tasks, which greatly affected my productivity at work. I kept switching jobs and departments. Every new job or department required learning new tasks. One of my jobs at the bank required me to travel around the country and give the same short talk to groups of three to ten people. I couldn't do it. I practiced the presentation over and over. I would go into an empty conference room and practice out loud. I stayed late at the office, working on this short talk that dealt in the general subject matter I had been trained in for twenty years. When it became clear I couldn't master this little presentation, I switched to a new company. And then, after a month at the new company, I tried to switch to another company that had also given me an offer. They turned me down. I am sure they thought I was nuts.

You might wonder how I could get so many job offers. In short, I was a great interviewer. I wore Brooks Brothers suits, Italian silk ties, and Ferragamo shoes. I could psyche myself up for any opportunity I thought would change my life. I looked good. I sounded good. I gave all the right answers. I could perform brilliantly for a thirty-minute interview. But with severe, chronic depression I couldn't perform effectively on any job.

With each job failure I sank further and further into the bowels of depression. By late 1999, I was a social recluse. The only escape from my misery was sleep. I lived to sleep. I got off work at 5:30 or 6:00 p.m. I would pick up some take-out food for a quick dinner. Then it was bedtime. I was often in bed by 7:00 or 7:30 and I would sleep straight through until 7:00 the next morning if it were a weekday. If it was the weekend, I could sleep fourteen hours straight. I hated the thought of getting out of bed and facing the world. Many sufferers of chronic depression hate mornings. It's an awful feeling.

The late 1990s weren't all work and sleep. I worked hard at clinging to the image that everything in my life was normal. For instance, my friends would invite me out to a movie and dinner. As soon as I was invited, panic would set in. I dreaded it. If I was invited on a Monday for a weekend movie, it was a long week. It's not possible to underestimate how stressful and how much energy it took me to go out for dinner and a movie. We'd see the movie and everyone else would talk about it at dinner. I couldn't concentrate enough to follow the plot, so I would sit in the movie theater for two hours, periodically looking at my watch, having little idea about the movie's main story line or even the names of the main characters. At dinner, I would nod my head periodically, acknowledging some particularly riveting scene that my dinner companions were talking about. And all the time I just wanted to get home as soon as possible, where I felt safe. The need to hide the hopelessness I felt left me feeling more isolated and consequently more depressed.

It was no way to live. I white-knuckled it seven days a week. Finally, thankfully, I couldn't work anymore. I say thankfully because quitting work stopped the downward spiral. I didn't stand a chance of getting better until the bleeding stopped. It was clear to my psychiatrist that I could not continue to work. Even my dad (the last holdout) finally said to me, "You're not going to make it if you don't give yourself a break."

O

chapter six

DO NOT DISTURB

I was now entering the third year of a major depressive episode. Isolation and social withdrawal, common symptoms of chronic depression, were a part of my life on a daily basis. However, in the normal course of events, there were many challenges to the "do not disturb" plan I had established. I wanted to perpetuate the appearance that everything was okay by fulfilling as many of my responsibilities as possible. On the other hand, there were things I was simply not well enough to do, which meant there was a constant tug-of-war going on between my outer persona and the reality of how ill I was inside.

The same week I had to take a medical leave of absence from work due to absolute physical and mental exhaustion, the battle was in full force. I received a telephone call from my brother in-law Russell. He told me he was giving my sister a surprise fortieth birthday party in December, with sixty or seventy people, at their home. Hmm. Seventy people crowded into a small living room, many of whom I had not seen in ten or twenty years, all asking me, "So, what are you doing now?" It just doesn't get any better than that!

I certainly wanted my sister to have a nice party, so the next day, during my weekly appointment with my psychologist, I threw myself on her mercy. I spent the next two months fretting about this surprise party on the couch in my psychologist's office. I wondered if I could attend the party. What would people think? What would I do? Go for an hour and then leave quietly? Go for half an hour and then excuse myself to go to another commitment? Stay for the entire party? It won't be as stressful as I am projecting it to be, right? Don't go at all? I discussed all these possibilities and everything in between. I felt if I attended the party, everyone would be staring at me and quizzing me about my life.

I did not decide what to do until forty-five minutes before the party. I made a last-minute beer run, blew up some balloons, hugged my brother in-law, and said, "I can't do it." Russell understood. My father concurred. I felt guilty, like a louse. But today I still stand by my decision. People who are ill (mentally or physically) do not belong at festive celebrations. I would share that same advice with anyone. Except . . .

In the summer of 2000 my phone rang with another challenge to my "do not disturb" plan. My dad said my other sister (who had surprisingly eloped with her longtime boyfriend) wanted a big wedding party in the fall, including a couple hundred guests, a band, a sit-down dinner—the whole works. Oh no, here we go again! But this time the choice was clearer; I couldn't NOT go to my sister's wedding party. Meanwhile, back on the psychologist's couch, the doctor had her work cut out for her.

The night of the party I was pumped. I drove to the club; pressed the elevator button for the twenty-third floor, and up I went. Twenty, twenty-one, twenty-two, and then the twenty-third floor. Ding. The doors opened and it was show time. It was a beautiful party, my sister was thrilled, and her friends were terrific. Even I could feel the joy and happiness. I did great, with just a few weak moments sprinkled in. But, man, it was hard work. When everyone was good and drunk, I found the elevator and departed. I felt like Rocky Balboa. I was so elated you could have peeled me off the ceiling. I was happy for my sister and her perfect party, and I gave myself a big pat on the back.

In early March 2001, the phone rang again. This time it was my sister-in-law Mary announcing a surprise fortieth birthday party for my brother. She said it would be great if I came, but no big deal. It was up to me. After the agony surrounding my sister's surprise party I had developed a rigid structure of systematically eliminating all unnecessary stress. I was in survival mode, in complete and utter despair, and I couldn't take it anymore. Sorry Michael, but I was a no-show at your party. He was so shocked by the surprise party, however, I'm sure he didn't notice my absence.

Two weeks after this party, I had the VNS implant procedure. Truly, though at this time in my life I simply wanted to die on the operating table. But as long as I was alive . . . I had to keep grinding away at keeping up the appearance of being a regular person. It was getting old. And I was getting tired.

My rigid structure of systematically eliminating all unnecessary stress was put to the test the next month when another one of my sisters called to say she wanted to throw Mom a surprise sixty-fifth birthday party in June. This was another event I could not imagine skipping. How can you miss your mother's sixty-fifth birthday party? You can't. I did everything in my power to make it as nice a party as possible. Once again, it was hard work to push myself forward while secretly not wanting to live. (My family was clueless as to my true state of mind.)

The party was wonderful. Mom was truly surprised, honored, and very happy to be the cause of this special occasion full of warmth and love. It even made a chronically depressed person happy. The only lesson learned in this situation had nothing to do with depression. It was that you should never plan a surprise birthday party with six siblings, each with conflicting ideas!

I wasn't only attending parties for other people. In 1998 I turned forty and had a party to celebrate. Even in the best of times, I never particularly liked celebrating my birthday. Fortunately this wasn't a surprise party with long-lost friends and acquaintances. It was a private dinner given by my parents at their home and attended only by my immediate and loving family. I remember the party because it was low-key and I was surrounded by the people who cared for me. My mother decorated the dining room table with a fortieth birthday theme. We had a wonderful dinner and a cake with candles, of course. I saved many of the decorations from the party.

Meanwhile, I had gained more than thirty pounds because I was sleeping an average of fourteen hours a day. Eating was one of my only pleasures and I did practically nothing active. I had tried exercising numerous times in the past. I knew it was a proven fact that exercise can elevate mood, and when I was younger I could play a couple of hours of tennis and then go for a run in 90-degree weather. The endorphins would kick in and I felt great. It was an emotional high, and I wanted to regain that feeling.

But no matter how hard and how often I exercised on the Stairmaster™, my mood never improved. No endorphins kicked in. Nothing. In fact, going to a public gym was horrifying. I remember walking into the room where the Stairmasters™ were

This sign greeted Charlie on his fortieth birthday party, held at his parents' house.

located, scared to death. The walls seemed fifty feet high. I felt panicky, self-conscious, and nervous. Everything about the experience was dismal. But I forced myself to spend thirty minutes on the Stairmaster™ as often as possible because everything I read said that exercise elevates mood.

Exercise did not work for me. I derived absolutely no relief from my depression, so I ultimately threw in the towel.

O

chapter seven

It's a Long New Year's Eve . . .

It's a long New Year's Eve that begins on the Fourth
of July. I disliked the Fourth of July for two reasons. First, it
reminded me of the fun holiday weekends I used to spend at the
beach every summer. In my childhood we would go to
Marblehead, Massachusetts, or Cape Cod. And when I was in my
twenties I spent time in the Hamptons at the eastern end of Long
Island. Secondly, Fourth of July meant the holiday season was fast
approaching.

Many people don't particularly enjoy the holiday season. It's
almost a cliché to complain about the holidays, but when someone suffers from chronic depression, the time between
Thanksgiving and New Year's Eve can be challenging. Although I
doubt many people start dreading the holidays in July.

The best time of the year for me was the second week of
January. The holidays were over and I had six months before July
Fourth.

The millennium was ushered in with little fanfare. I was on an
unpaid medical leave of absence from work. I had friends who

celebrated the turn of the century with magnificent trips, parties, and extravaganzas. I could have cared less. I was in bed by 9:00 p.m. But most importantly, my boss wasn't beating me up and I wasn't suffering total mental and physical exhaustion from the daily pressure of trying to learn new material for my latest job change (August 1999). It was a tremendous relief. The relief far outweighed the loss of income. I now had a chance to heal, recover, and regroup; something that was impossible under all of the stress I had existed under the previous five years. Quitting work ultimately proved to be the right way to start the twenty-first century.

I recently read an article about phobias. It contained brief descriptions about cynophobia (fear of dogs), clourophoia (fear of clowns), and five or six other phobias. I found my phobia, or rather my former phobia. I never knew it had a name: *agoraphobia.* The article did a great job of explaining phobias. Here is what it said:

> Phobias may be irrational, but they are also very real. Agoraphobia, which is a fear of public places, can rule a victim's life. The National Institute of Mental Health estimates that 5.1 to 12.5 percent of Americans suffer from phobias. Phobias are estimated to be the most common psychiatric illness among women of any age, and the second most common among men over 25.
>
> Agoraphobia is generally interpreted as a fear of public places and a fear of being unable to escape the situation. This is the most common and the most debilitating phobia. It can cripple someone and greatly affect their life.
>
> *St. Louis Post Dispatch*, April 26, 2004

It seems I always have the most debilitating of anything! This described me perfectly. I was fearful every time I left my home. My home was my nest. It was where I felt safest. I did not have to struggle to keep up appearances. Anything that involved leaving my "nest" was stressful.

Although I live less than two miles from the largest shopping mall in St. Louis, The Galleria, it was the last place I would go to shop. Why? Because it would be the most likely place I would see people I knew and hadn't seen in one, two, five, or ten years. I didn't want to put on a happy face and make small talk. I certainly didn't want to say, "I'm in my third year of a major depressive episode. How are you doing?"

If I needed to go to a mall, I drove fifteen miles from home, minimizing the chance for an unwanted encounter. If I *had* to go to The Galleria for something, I took all the shortcuts and would actually run into the mall, make my purchase, and run out again. My heart would be pounding and I would be sweating because I was so scared. I couldn't get home fast enough.

This pattern was repeated over and over, whether it was the grocery story or the post office. It didn't matter. Anywhere but home was difficult for me.

The best description of me at this time is that I was a mental vegetable, a shut-in. I lived in a prison without bars. I wasn't working. I had no outside interests, no hobbies, and hadn't read a book or seen a movie in a long time. When I did have to engage in social conversation with a friend or a relative who knew about my personal situation, I tried to be empathetic. They were in a difficult situation as well; it's tough having a conversation with the equivalent of a doorknob. But overall, most people were exceedingly gracious and kind to me. Nobody asked intrusive questions, and the conversation was generally kept light. They did everything they could to make me feel comfortable and at ease. I did the same for them. And I continued the charade that everything was hunky dory.

Meanwhile my immediate family wondered what the hell was going on. They were in an impossible situation. As far as they could tell I was fine. I looked good and sounded good, so why wasn't I back to leaping tall buildings? By perpetuating this cover-up, I confused the hell out of everyone and ultimately made life more difficult for myself. The better I tried to look on the outside, the worse I felt on the inside, further baffling everyone around me, and increasing my need to isolate myself.

My family (like the rest of the world) did not understand the disease of depression or, more specifically, chronic depression. They wondered about me constantly. Is he really better? If so, then he needs to get his shit together. Maybe he's not better, now what do we do? Is it live or is it Memorex? They could not comprehend how I could exist the way I was living. They wanted to fix what was broken so that I could live a happy life.

But no one knew what to do. I could go away for a couple of months to a place like The Menninger Clinic in Topeka, Kansas (now in Houston, Texas), or McLean Hospital in Boston. There was an alternative institution in Arizona or New Mexico. But I felt in my gut there was nothing any of these facilities could do for me. My family wanted me to seriously consider this for a solution. I had done a lot of research on the subject, and had a stack of marketing brochures. I came close to entering one of those places, but in the end I didn't and I am convinced it would not have worked.

My family was totally frustrated and confused. I had promised myself I would never lie to my family when asked a question. After a while, however, I started to run out of tactful ways to tell them I was dead from the neck up and in a continuous state of utter despair.

"Oh, I had an uneventful day," I would say.

"And then what did you do after that?" they would ask.

I eventually ran out of answers. How many ways could I tell them I hadn't done anything? I felt like a spin doctor, trying to put my best face on everything.

Social isolation, withdrawal, and loss of interest in the outside world are textbook symptoms of depression. I think my family thought if they encouraged me to get out, attend parties, watch football and hockey games, etc., I would be cured. Wrong!

I am not a mental health professional, but I can say that if you are suffering from severe depression and agoraphobia (fear of public places) there is no worse place to be than a big party or a crowded seventy-thousand seat stadium filled with screaming drunks.

But I did these and other similar things to please my family and friends. I know they meant well, but it is like telling a person with a broken leg to go for a two-mile jog around the track because it will be good for them. It won't help the broken leg to run for two miles, and it doesn't help a depressed person with agoraphobia to go out into public when they are not ready to do so.

I developed a herniated disc two years ago. One simple piece of advice the physical therapist gave me was: "If something doesn't feel good or aggravates the pain in your back, don't do it!" Sadly this common-sense advice is not dispensed to people with a mental illness. I was a people pleaser and I did what other people thought was good for me, no matter how painful it was. Every time I subjected myself to additional mental stress or discomfort, it took me down a notch.

In essence, I felt worthless, guilty, sad, hopeless, and fatigued. I could not concentrate, follow a conversation, or experience pleasure. My misery was unending.

Chronic depression continues without interruption. No one can fix chronic depression, not the doctors, not you. And everybody gets frustrated. My strategy was to never miss a dose of medication, a psychotherapy appointment, or an appointment with my psychiatrist. I continued to hope that something would break my way.

O

chapter eight

A GLIMMER OF LIGHT

On Tuesday, October 23, 2000, I felt particularly desperate during my regular therapy session with my psychologist. I didn't know what to do. My entire body ached. I sat on the edge of the couch, hands clutched, pleading, "You've just got to help me. What's going to happen to me? What kind of future do I have? How do I get out of this mental hellhole?"

I had been seeing this psychologist for several years; initially on a weekly basis; now every two weeks. I never missed an appointment. My only hope of getting better was to stick to a strict treatment plan. I hoped that maybe I would get a lucky break and get better. I got the first hint of a fluky break that day.

During our session, the psychologist casually mentioned she had recently read something about vagus nerve stimulation and depression in *TIME* or *Newsweek* magazine. (I had never heard of the vagus nerve.) She couldn't remember any of the details from the article. We looked through some magazines in her waiting room, but couldn't find the article. I said I would ask my psychiatrist about it at my next scheduled office visit. Then I went straight to the periodical's section of the local library. After an hour of skimming magazines, I found the article about vagus nerve stimulation and epilepsy. The last sentence of the article casually mentioned that stimulation of the vagus nerve might have some implications for sufferers of chronic depression. I hmm

. . .

On Thursday, November 2, 2000, I met with my psychiatrist. As I sat in the waiting room, I thought about all the times over the past couple of years that I had squirmed in my chair, asking myself: "What am I going to say to this guy? It's always doom and gloom." His compassion, patience, understanding of depression, and incredible insight into what was going on in my mind was remarkable. He listened carefully; he didn't talk a lot during a session, but when it was his time to speak, the information was golden. No condescending platitudes; only measured guidance and support. I always left his office feeling encouraged to keep on going. At the end of this visit, I asked him if he had heard anything about vagus nerve stimulation and depression. He told me he had and that St. Louis University (SLU) was going to be involved in the investigational clinical trial.

Ironically, St. Louis University was only ten minutes from where I lived! I was determined to find out more about the clinical trial. There was something about the word *investigational* that implied aggressive to me. I liked the sound of it. If it's aggressive, it must be good. I paid the receptionist and drove home. As soon as I walked in the door, I picked up the phone and dialed 411. I asked for the telephone number for St. Louis University. After a short pause I heard, "Press the number one and the call will be automatically dialed. An additional charge will apply." Who cares? I pressed the number one before the recording could finish.

The university operator had trouble connecting me with anyone who had heard of this procedure. I was passed around from department to department, including one that experimented on rats and mice (I knew I must be getting closer!). Eventually I reached the Department of Psychiatry, and then, finally, the Clinical Trials Unit within the Department of Psychiatry, where I left a message with the receptionist. I wasn't sure whether I had reached a dead end. Miraculously I got a call from a psychiatric nurse, JoAnn Filla Taylor, RN, the next day. She conducted a pre-screening telephone interview to determine if I would be a suitable candidate for the next stage of pre-qualification. She scheduled me for more interviews, including a meeting with the psychiatrist who was the lead investigator for the study at St. Louis University (SLU), Charles F. Conway, MD.

On Monday, November 20, 2000, in the Clinical Trials Unit of the Department of Psychiatry at SLU, I was interviewed by several people; filled out many forms, surveys, and depression rating questionnaires; and provided my medical history, including medications, hospitalizations, and doctors' names and addresses. It was not a simple process; I didn't just walk in the door and say I'd like to volunteer for the investigational clinical trial. I had to qualify to be included as a study patient. And these interviews and questionnaires were only the beginning.

The study investigators had to independently verify each piece of information. They required records from doctors and hospitals going back many years to verify that I had indeed tried all available treatments for depression and that all the treatments had failed. The interviews were unusual. I wasn't sure what type of person they were looking for and they were somewhat vague about exactly what it took to get in. I guess that was part of the study design. It was definitely not like interviewing for a prime-time TV reality show, where you pretty much know what the producers are looking for. I had the feeling they weren't looking for the "Joe Millionaire" type or even "Average Joe," but more like "Joe Defeated." I don't mean to use the word "defeated" in a derogatory manner, rather I use it to describe the losing battle I was experiencing with depression. After all, every available medical therapy (pharmaceuticals, ECT, psychotherapy) had failed me. I also had the sense they wanted someone who was motivated to get better.

The exact criteria for inclusion in the study have not yet been published. However, a summary of the characteristics of the study patients is shown in the following sidebar. These characteristics are derived by using the Hamilton Rating Scale for Depression (see Appendix I). These were patients suffering from an episode of severe depression that had lasted for an average of four years, with a total of twenty-five years of depression over their lifetimes! No other trial ever studied such a severely depressed patient population.

Patient Characteristics in Clinical Trial	Evaluable Population (205 patients)
Average Age(years)	46
% of Female Patients	64%
Average Baseline Depression Rating	Moderate to severe
Average Duration of Lifetime Illness	25
Average Duration, Current Episode (years)	4.2
% Treated with ECT in Current Episode	35%
Reference: Cyberonics Presentation to FDA Advisory Panel on June 15, 2004.	

The study was a double-blind placebo-controlled study, which meant I had a 50 percent chance of *not* receiving treatment (stimulation to my vagus nerve) until after I had completed the short-term phase of the study. In a double-blind study, neither the doctors nor patients know who is receiving the treatment. Even though I would be implanted with the device, there was a 50 percent chance it wouldn't be turned on right away, although even patients in the placebo group would eventually have the device turned on. That was the deal. Take it or leave it.

I desperately wanted to know what the odds were of getting relief from my depression. And that's the question they couldn't answer. This was truly a pioneering experimental study, so nobody had the answer. The doctor's response to my question about what were the odds that vagus nerve stimulation could help me was cautious and measured. He said there was an *inkling* there may be something to this.

I said to myself, "*Inkling?* I'll take an inkling. An *inkling* was all I needed to agree to the procedure." I had tried everything else. As long as the procedure was safe, which it is, I had nothing to lose. And I suspect that many desperate patients will feel the same way. But now, people will have the benefit of knowing that vagus nerve stimulation is much more than just an inkling, it has been proven to positively affect the areas of the brain that modulate mood and depression.

I had other questions, too:

Is VNS related in any way to ECT?

No, there is no relationship between ECT and vagus nerve stimulation. ECT induces a grand mal seizure, which alters many chemical aspects of the brain during and after seizure activity.

How big are the scars?

The nurse held up two fingers about an inch apart. (She was off by about two inches.)

What's the downside risk?

It might not work, but I would be no worse off than I was now.

How long is the recovery?

Not very long.

Is there any monetary compensation for being a study patient?

No, there was no financial compensation.

The clinical trial had two hundred patients from twenty different hospitals throughout the United States. If I did the math correctly, that meant only ten patients would be implanted at the St. Louis University study site. This made me nervous. It felt like I was in a competition. I hoped I could I get approved fast enough, before all ten slots had been filled.

Over the next few months, I had more interviews with the study investigators. All of my medical records from psychiatrists and hospitals from the last fifteen years had to be reviewed. Then the waiting game began. I would call JoAnn every couple of weeks to see if I had been approved or qualified. "Nothing has been decided," is all that she was authorized to say. There was nothing I could do to improve my chances of being accepted into the trial study.

My family kept asking me what was going on. Even though nobody knew what the procedure was about, they desperately wanted me to have it done. Since I could get no information from SLU, there was nothing I could tell my family. It was a waiting game.

In early February 2001, I made my regular phone call to JoAnn. She told me that a file from one doctor was missing. That doctor's office said they had sent it, but JoAnn never received it. I was determined to be included as a subject for the clinical trial and was not going to let the U.S. Postal Service screw it up. So I got in the car, drove to the doctor's office, picked up the information, and then hand delivered the sealed envelope to JoAnn. Even after personally handing the envelope to JoAnn, I left her office with absolutely no clue as to whether I would be considered a candidate.

Finally, one day in early March, the phone rang. It was JoAnn. "You're in!" she said. I had no idea what I was in for—but I was in! The SLU study investigators had approved me. My information was forwarded to Cyberonics, the manufacturer of the vagus nerve stimulator, where the researchers had given the final approval for me to be included in the study. I was relieved. I was going to get the chance to try a new treatment that could potentially give me some relief from my chronic despair. That's all I wanted, an opportunity, something to hope for, the possibility of improving the quality of my life. I felt like a high school senior who had just gotten accepted into Princeton after being on the waiting list for four months.

During my regularly scheduled office visit on Tuesday March 19, 2001, I told my psychiatrist I had been accepted into the study. I asked him if he thought I should go ahead with the procedure. There was little to discuss. We spent less than five minutes on the subject. The doctor politely suggested I talk it over with my family. We had reached a point where there was absolutely nothing to lose. I'm sure he was thinking I had better go for it and let the chips fall where they may!

I completed the pre-surgery preliminaries, including a couple of office visits with the neurosurgeon, Dr. Richard Bucholz. The implant procedure was scheduled to take place on April 4, 2001. It would be an inpatient overnight hospital stay. On Monday, April 2, 2001, I completed the final round of tests and questionnaires about my depression and related symptoms. I met with my rater—Raymond Tait, PhD, Director of Clinical Trials in the Department of Psychiatry at SLU—the doctor who would meet with me weekly to assess my depression during the short-term part of the study, which would last twelve weeks. He did not know whether I was assigned to the treatment group or the placebo group.

This meeting was to establish the baseline level of my depression. I won't bore you with the details of the numerous questions I had to answer; but I want you to know how depressed I was. I told Dr. Tait I wanted to die on the operating table. I knew the surgery was simple and there was little chance of anything going wrong, but I hoped something inexplicable would happen. If I died during surgery then all of my problems would be solved--it would be the ultimate escape. (Clearly I had nowhere to go but up from that level of depression.)

I felt incredible pressure in the days leading up to the surgery. I believed that if I didn't wake up completely cured I would once again be considered a failure.

The routine procedure was performed on Wednesday, April 4. It is surgery, performed by surgeons in an operating room. Fortunately I had no physical problems (high blood pressure, diabetes, heart disease, allergies, etc.) to potentially complicate the procedure. (More detailed information about the implant is provided in the appendices.)

You should feel no pressure about having this surgery, in fact just the opposite. Researchers know that improvement in mood occurs gradually, over time. Progress should be measured in calendar quarters, not weeks. (I elaborate on this later in the book.)

My parents drove me to the hospital at 6:00 in the morning. We checked in and went to the operating area. I put on a hospital gown, a nurse stuck an IV in me, and my parents and I watched the *Today Show* for an hour and a half. My dad gave me one good piece of advice: make sure you ask for something to calm your nerves before surgery. The anesthesiologist obliged. I hugged my dad. I hugged my mom. I was wheeled away for surgery. My parents left for a sumptuous breakfast in the hospital cafeteria.

In the operating room the Chief Neurosurgery Resident

greeted me. The anesthesiologist put me to sleep. A stimulator was implanted in my upper left chest; two lead wires from the stimulator were tunneled under my skin and wrapped around the left vagus nerve in my neck. The surgeon's knife never went above the fold in the lowest part of my neck.

The implant procedure is relatively simple. Surgeons have been doing chest implants since 1958 and this identical procedure has been performed safely on more than 30,000 epilepsy patients since 1997. However, you certainly want the surgeon to pay attention when he coils the lead wire around your vagus nerve!

I strongly recommend that patients choose a surgeon who has specific experience operating within the carotid sheath. The vagus nerve lies deep and in between the common carotid artery and the jugular vein. This is the most critical part of the procedure.

Steven C. Schacter and Dieter Schmidt, *Vagus Nerve Stimulation, Second Edition*, 2003. Martin Dunitz.

The surgery was uneventful. It was over before lunchtime. My parents and JoAnn were waiting for me. The neurosurgeon told them everything went fine, no problems. My parents tried to find out from JoAnn whether I would be assigned to the treatment group and what was the probability of success. They had no luck in getting an answer from her. I was happy my parents met JoAnn, because they had a chance to pick her brain. They quickly discovered the study investigators were not divulging any information that would compromise the study. People suffering from chronic depression are often accused of keeping secrets. My family thought I had been deliberately withholding information from them. It was nice to have third-party verification I wasn't hiding anything about the treatment. I think my dad summed it up best when he said he couldn't get a thing (information) out of that broad (JoAnn)!

The neurosurgeon stopped by later in the afternoon; while I was being catheterized no less. I saw him a week later for a quick checkup for scars. I haven't seen him since. I wouldn't know what he looked like if I bumped into him on the street. He did a great job. The scars healed beautifully. His job was done.

O
chapter nine

I'VE BEEN IMPLANTED, NOW WHAT?

You will have many questions when you consider this surgery. Although I had no answers before my surgery; I want you to have the benefit of my experience.

How bad is the pain?

During the twelve hours post surgery I mostly slept, due to the anesthesia. I felt minor soreness and stiffness around the implant. I could definitely feel the implant under the skin of my upper left chest. I was extremely hoarse. My throat was sore from the intubation tube used during surgery. The doctor prescribed Tylenol™ with codeine—none of the good stuff like Vicodin™ or OxyContin™! I needed the pain medication for about three days after the surgery. I kept thinking to myself, I just had surgery, shouldn't I be in more pain? But I wasn't.

What do the scars look like?

Since I didn't have a camera crew waiting for me as I exited the recovery room, I don't have pictures of the fresh scars. But those would be irrelevant.

In the weeks following the surgery, I was surprised by the size of the scar on my neck. It was bigger than I had expected; it was four inches long and swollen. If you're a man and have to shave around the bottom of your neck, you will have to be careful for a month. If you're a woman and you have to shave around the bottom of your neck, I can't help you.

Since I was implanted Cyberonics has introduced a revised model of the stimulator, Model 102, which is 30 percent smaller and has 46 percent less volume than its predecessor. It also has one lead wire rather than two. This means that the procedure should now cause less scarring than I experienced, and the neurosurgeon has only one lead to coil around the vagus nerve. Cyberonics has announced they will have Model 103 available in 2006, a smaller version than Model 102 that offers enhanced functionality for the surgeon as well as increased options for setting the stimulation parameters of the device.

After healing, the scars are minor. I have included several pictures on the following pages, taken by a professional photographer, of the scar on my neck and the scar on my upper left chest. (They say a picture is worth a thousand words, and these pictures should make anyone feel comfortable that he or she could live with this minor scar, even if they derived no benefit whatsoever from the device.

After these pictures were taken, I sent them to my editor, Roxann Schroeder, PhD and to the book packager who would create my book in e-book and paperback formats, Mary Jo

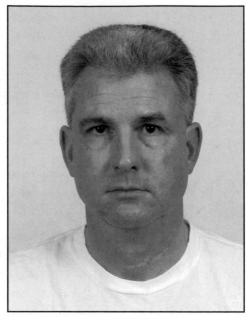

Scar on neck.

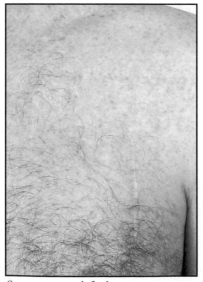

Scar on upper left chest.

With a suit and tie on, the scars are unnoticeable.

Zazueta. I wanted to know right away if there would be any issues with the pictures, so we had time to correct the problem before publication. Mary Jo said there must have been trouble with the lighting or the photographer's lens because she could hardly see the scars, especially the one on my upper left chest. However, these pictures are an accurate portrayal of the scars. When I go for a regular physical my primary care physician has difficulty finding the scar on my chest. Since the new stimulators are 30 percent smaller, scars in the future should be even less.

I included the picture of me wearing a tie to show that the scar on the fold of the neck is completely hidden. Roxann pointed out that it would be helpful to have a picture of a woman to show that the scar would not be disfiguring for females either. This brought up another interesting point. One of the rules of the study was we were not allowed to meet or communicate with any other study patient. I have never met or spoken to another patient in the study. So, unless I dressed up in drag, it would be difficult to get a picture of a woman. Sorry about that!

How long does it take to recover?

Not long. I don't remember being given any specific instructions. Obviously, if you still have anesthesia in your system, you shouldn't drive or operate heavy machinery. I have never operated heavy machinery in my life, and I just took it easy for three or four days at my parent's house.

I was still suffering from severe depression. I want to clarify that the post-surgery recovery and the depression recovery are two separate issues.

The meat of the study began on Monday, April 9, five days after the implant. There were two phases to the study, the short-term phase and the long-term phase. The short-term phase was scheduled to last for three months post-surgery. For some patients the short-term phase lasted six months.

Every week for twelve weeks I met with JoAnn. I placed a programmable wand over the area of the implant. The wand was connected to a laptop computer. (Today they use a Palm Pilot.) She pressed a couple of buttons on the computer, the computer made a few noises, then she gave me the okay to put down the wand. This procedure turned off the device for the patients in the treatment group, but the same procedure had to be followed with the placebo group as well, so that no one knew what group he or she was in.

The next step was a two-hour interview and depression-rating session with my rater, Dr. Tait, who also did not know which group I was in. I answered the same questions every week. Even under the best of circumstances this would be a grind, but I had severe hoarseness (more on that later) and no relief from the depression. The interviews became tedious and frustrating.

After our meetings, Dr. Tait would complete a separate questionnaire on his observations about me. I headed back to JoAnn's office, where there was another questionnaire waiting for me. This one I completed by myself in her office. It was a thirty-question multiple-choice questionnaire titled "Inventory of Depressive Symptomatology." Then I placed the programmable wand over the area of the implant. Once again, the computer made a few noises and she would give the signal to put down the wand.

Here is an example of one of the questions in the self-questionnaire, "Inventory of Depressive Symptomatology." Some of the questions were a bit tricky to answer, but this one was always the easiest:

Question 17. View of My Future
___ 0 I have an optimistic view of my future

___1 I am occasionally pessimistic about my future, but for the most part I believe things will get better.

___2 I am pretty certain that my immediate future (1-2 months) does not hold much promise of good things for me.

___3 I see no hope of anything good happening to me any time in the future.

For many months my answer was always the same: #3. I had absolutely no hope about my future. Gradually, my answer changed to #2, and then #1. For the past three years, my answer has been #0. I do not have to cheat in order to answer that I have an optimistic view of my future. (It's a wonderful feeling.)

Then JoAnn got her chance to ask questions. Her job was to monitor any changes in my physical health, medications, and dosages. If I had taken anything new (even Tylenol™) she needed to know the exact date I started the medication and when I discontinued taking it. Did I have any new physical problems? How was the hoarseness? The whole process was meticulous. But, even after all this, I still wasn't done for the day.

The last meeting was always with a psychiatrist. It was a short meeting. He reviewed the information I had given to JoAnn and asked a few questions. By that time, I was more than ready to leave. There was never any variation in the process, the order of the interviews, or the precise nature of the visits. Week after week it was always the same. I stopped counting after a while. I just did what I was told.

Three years after my implant surgery these visits still continue, although only on a quarterly basis. The process is the same, except we skip the sham part of the process, since I have been *unblinded.* I also complete the self-assessment questionnaire every month. JoAnn phones to notify me it's time to do the questionnaire, which we now, thankfully, do over the phone. I do not know the date my stimulator was turned on or how and when it was ramped up to toleration. They say they may never be allowed to tell me. At this point, I don't care. The device proved effective for me, that is all I need to know!

In addition to the main study, there were several optional parts to it. I agreed to give periodic blood samples and to have PET scans. A positron emission tomography (PET) scan is an imaging technique that uses positively charged particles to detect subtle changes in the body's metabolism and chemical activities. It provides a color-coded image of the body's function, rather than its structure. Medical specialists are just beginning to discover how PET scans can be used to evaluate a wide range of patients, including psychiatric patients. I hope my participation in this part of the study was helpful. I did not agree to have my interviews videotaped. No thanks. (This may prove to be a wise decision. I am writing this as Jay Leno is making jokes about Paris Hilton's secret sex video. What if I somehow became rich and famous? You know the tapes would surface. No thank you.)

I was a good patient. I never missed an appointment for blood work, PET scans, interviews, or physicals. I did everything I was told.

Even after a month the hoarseness was not lessening. There was no pain; just severe hoarseness. And every week, the study investigators would nod their heads sympathetically but said nothing. Their silence was deafening. I wanted to know more.

On Tuesday, May 8, 2001, I made an appointment with an Ear, Nose and Throat specialist at Barnes Hospital in St. Louis. "Squeeze this," he said, handing me a ball of gauze. "You might feel some discomfort." He stuck a scope through my nose and down to my throat so that he could see my vocal cords. Whenever a doctor says you may feel some discomfort, you know you're in trouble.

"Your left vocal cord is not moving," he said. After thinking about it for a couple of minutes he said, "I've never heard of this crazy procedure. But if I were you, I would just let Mother Nature take her course. I think over time, you'll be fine." It turns out he gave me good advice.

Little by little, the hoarseness lessened. There was substantial improvement three to four months after the implant, when it was impossible to differentiate the hoarseness from the initial surgery and the hoarseness that resulted from the activation of the stimulator. It is important to note that while some patients have hoarseness or voice alteration from the device activating, these side effects dissipate over time. I have no voice alteration anymore, nor do I feel anything when the stimulator is activated. The only way I know for sure that the device is working is when JoAnn checks the settings.

───────────────────────

Less than 1 percent of the patients in the study had temporary left vocal cord paralysis after surgery. I mention it because it happened to me. Hoarseness was a side effect of the surgery in 68 percent of the patients, but it dissipated over time, and the length of time varied with each patient. Meanwhile, the benefits of stimulation kicked in gradually. In my opinion, if you have suffered from chronic depression for many years, then a few months of tolerable side effects should not deter you from considering this procedure.

───────────────────────

I don't know when my stimulator was turned on. I learned in November 2003 I was assigned to the treatment group from day one, but because of my severe hoarseness the device was not turned on or ramped up until the hoarseness settled down. I do not know what level the device is currently set at. The study investigators say I may never be told.

At some point (probably late summer 2001) I began to notice a slight tickle in my throat. It was minor and increased the hoarseness a bit. I assumed this was a sign that the stimulator had been activated. The device settings vary with each individual, but a common setting would be thirty seconds of stimulation every five minutes, twenty-four hours a day, seven days a week. The patient does not need to do anything; compliance is guaranteed.

By the late fall, there was minor improvement in my mood. It was subtle, but noticeable.

Wednesday, December 5, 2001, was the day before my regular appointment with my psychiatrist. I remember it distinctly. I carefully laid out the clothes I was going to wear to the appointment. I am sure the doctor thought I owned only one pair of jeans, one shirt, and a pair of tennis shoes. But something inside me wanted me to look good for this appointment. I can't explain it. I found a beautiful cashmere sweater from Saks that I hadn't worn in years, a pair of Italian dress cords, and a starched white shirt. I shined my loafers.

Before depression took over my life, I had taken a lot of pride in the way I dressed. Pulling out nice clothes must sound woefully minor to anyone who has never suffered from chronic depression, but those who suffer can fully appreciate this tiny victory. I told my psychiatrist I lived a quiet, solitary life, which was okay with me. It was not a life most other people would want. But it was an improvement over mental turmoil, which was a huge improvement for me.

The neurosurgeon who performed the implant procedure wanted me to schedule an appointment with him nine months after the surgery, due to the severe hoarseness that was evident a week after the implant. Since the hoarseness eventually improved significantly, I didn't feel like going to another appointment. I was tired of seeing doctors. There would have been little to talk about. On Sunday, January 20, 2002, I wrote him a letter requesting a cancellation of the appointment.

Dr. Bucholz wrote back and agreed an appointment was unnecessary. He also said the mild hoarseness and scarring would continue to lessen over time.

O

chapter ten

If At First You Don't Succeed . . .

On Tuesday, January 22, 2002, Cyberonics, Inc.
issued a significant press release. It is important you fully understand its contents as it has essential implications about the Vagus
Nerve Stimulation Therapy's potential success or failure in
patients. There might be some propaganda and false rumors (via
the internet, uniformed physicians, etc.) about the results of the
short-term part of the study. I have tried to dissect the ramifica-
tions of the press release for you, so you will know and
understand the correct facts.

In any investigational study, whether for a new drug or for a
medical device, there may be mistakes or shortcomings in the
study design. If you are a huge drug company like Merck, with
over $15 billion in annual revenues, these types of oversights don't
become a momentous event and are often hidden from the public. But if you are a one-product medical device company, with
about $100 million in annual revenues, such events are signifi-
cant.

PRESS RELEASE

HOUSTON, January 22, 2002 /PRNewswire-FirstCall/ - Cyberonics, Inc. (Nasdaq: CYBX) today announced acute results in the pivotal depression study (D-02) assessing the efficacy of Vagus Nerve Stimulation Therapy (VNS Therapy(TM)) in 235 people with chronic or recurrent depression. There were no statistically significant differences found when 12-week acute treatment and placebo group response and remission rates were compared. A thorough review of all acute data and long-term data is underway. Preliminary review of the treatment group stimulation parameters suggests that over 50% of the patients in the treatment group received insufficient stimulation to derive benefit from VNS Therapy.

"Cyberonics was initially surprised by these acute depression pivotal study results considering the encouraging acute and long-term data from the 60-patient study and the depression mechanism of action findings," commented Robert P. Cummings, Cyberonics' Chairman and Chief Executive Officer. "Our preliminary detailed review of the acute and long-term data from the study suggests that response and remission rates improve over time similar to what was seen in the pilot study, but that inconsistent with our previous epilepsy and depression studies, over 50% of the patients in the treatment group may have been under-stimulated and did not receive efficacious does of VNS Therapy during the entire 10-week acute treatment period. Our clinical development team led by Richard L. Rudolph, M.D., Vice President of Clinical and Medical Affairs & Chief Medical Officer, is rapidly completing their review of the pivotal study results. At this point, it appears as though we will: 1) request an amendment to the D-02 protocol to require adequate doses of VNS Therapy during the long-term follow-up phase of the study, and 2) request approval to convert our conditionally-approved 550-patient Phase IIIB D-08 protocol into a 300-patient 6-month

randomized, double-blind, placebo-controlled confirmatory pivotal study to prove that VNS Therapy is an effective
and tolerable long-term maintenance therapy for patients
with chronic or recurrent depression."

Dr. Rudolph added, "Although we are disappointed in
the acute study results, it is noteworthy that approximately
50% of clinical trials submitted in recent antidepressant
New Drug Applications were failed trials. Our preliminary
review suggests that the lack of a significant difference
between treatment and placebo groups represents a
failed study, not a failure of the therapy. We remain confident in the unique value of VNS Therapy as a treatment for
depression. Although our depression PMA-S submission
may be delayed for two or three years, when it is submitted, it will be supported by compelling long-term clinical
evidence that VNS Therapy is an effective and tolerable
long-term maintenance therapy which could benefit up
to 4 million people with chronic or recurrent depression.
The need is still there and the VNS Therapy investigators
and patients are still enthusiastic. We expect that we will
have FDA approval for our new protocol by June 2002."

# #

Let me clarify what happened, by translating several statements from the press release into plain English.

"Cyberonics today announced acute results in the pivotal depression study assessing the efficacy of Vagus Nerve Stimulation Therapy in 235 people with chronic or recurrent depression."

Translation: *Acute* simply means the short-term part of the study. The twelve-week acute period of the study consisted of three parts: a two-week post-operation recovery period, a two-week period of ramping up the stimulation level, and an eight-week "fixed" level of vagus nerve stimulation.

Pivotal means it is a test to determine if the device works. The purpose of a pivotal trial is to confirm efficacy, patient tolerability, and to monitor adverse reactions. Without efficacy, you can't go to the FDA for approval. Tolerability and adverse reactions information is needed to evaluate the overall benefit-risk relationship of the device and to provide a basis for labeling guidelines (if approved by the FDA). Ironically, safety and tolerability have never been an issue with the device.

To be considered pivotal, a study must:

- Be controlled, using a placebo or a standard therapy as a control condition to compare the treatment results
- Have a double-blind design (neither the patient nor the investigators know if the patient is in the placebo or treatment group) when such a design is practical and ethical. Be randomized—the patients are assigned to the placebo or treatment group randomly
- Be of adequate size--there are enough patients to get a statistically relevant result

A randomized study is not required for medical device investigational trials.

"There were no statistically significant differences found when ten-week acute treatment and placebo group response and remission rates were compared"

Translation: The short-term study failed. *Response* to the device means patients who reported a 50 percent or greater improvement in their depression; *remission* implies a complete recovery.

"A thorough review of all acute (short-term) data and long-term data is underway."

Translation: What the hell went wrong? You can safely assume that there was some sort of turmoil going on at company headquarters. Clearly this was a setback for Cyberonics, but more importantly, it was a major blow to the millions of patients (and their families) that could have benefited from the device.

"Preliminary review of the treatment group stimulation parameters suggests that over 50 percent of the patients in the treatment group received insufficient stimulation to derive benefit from VNS Therapy."

Translation: Apparently the design of the study protocol did not require the investigators at the twenty study sites to ramp up the treatment group patients to an efficacious level of stimulation. Consequently, more than 50 percent of the patients in the treatment group didn't get a therapeutic level of stimulation. "More than 50 percent" could mean 51 percent or it could mean 80 percent. We'll never know.

"Cyberonics was initially surprised by these acute depression pivotal study results considering the encouraging acute and long-term data from the sixty-patient pilot study (from 1998) and the depression mechanism of actions findings."

Translation: *Surprised* was probably the understatement of the year. The patients in the pilot study, as well as thousands of epilepsy patients implanted with the device, had reported an improvement in mood. There was clearly conflicting data in the pivotal study when compared to previous outcomes.

"Our preliminary detailed review of the acute and long-term data from the study suggests that response and remission rates improve over time similar to what was seen in the pilot study; over 50 percent of the patients in the treatment group may have been under-stimulated and did not receive efficacious doses of the VNS Therapy during the entire ten-week acute period."

Translation: The initial design of the study was flawed. This was a pioneering study. Everyone learned important information about how the device works. The acute study failed because patients did not get a therapeutic level of stimulation, but vagus nerve stimulation therapy is not a failure.

"Our preliminary detailed review of the acute and long-term data was similar to what was seen in the pilot studies; over 50 percent of the patients in the treatment group may have been under-stimulated and did not receive efficacious doses of VNS Therapy during the ten-week acute treatment period."

Translation: When the device is first turned on, it is set to 0.25 milliamps, the lowest possible setting. The highest setting is 3.0 milliamps. While the minimum effective level of stimulation has yet to be determined, the best guess is somewhere between 1.0 milliamps and 1.25 milliamps. It turns out that at least 50 percent of the patients in the treatment group had the device turned on, but were never ramped up to an effective level of stimulation. It is like going into a windowless, pitch-black basement and turning on the dimmer switch to the lowest level, then coming back in eight weeks to see if the light has gotten any brighter. It doesn't work that way.

"At this point, it appears as though we will: 1) request an amendment to the D-02* protocol to require adequate doses of therapy during the long-term follow-up phase of the study, and 2) request approval to convert our conditionally-approved 550-patient Phase IIIB D-08 protocol into a 300-patient 6-month randomized, double-blind, placebo-controlled confirmatory study to prove that VNS Therapy is an effective and tolerable long-term maintenance therapy for patients with chronic or recurrent depression." (D-02 is the official name of the investigational study.)

Translation: This is an important statement for a number of reasons. First of all, it's always a good idea to give patients the correct dosage of therapy. One of the options that Cyberonics was apparently considering was a 550-patient study with a six-month acute period. This would have required 550 chronically depressed people to agree to the implant procedure, knowing they only had a 50 percent chance of having the stimulator turned on for six months. I doubt that would have been easy. Moreover, it was an acknowledgement that it takes time before the patient begins to feel the benefits.

If you think about it logically, what would you rather have: a short-term response (eight weeks) to a treatment or a sustained response that lasted for eight, eighteen, thirty-six or more months? I have experienced a sustained response for almost thirty-six months.

It also highlighted a flaw in the design of the pivotal study, with its eight-week fixed dosage of VNS. On average, the patients in this study had suffered twenty-five years of lifetime depression. Twenty-five years! And the average length of the current episode was 4.1 years. The treatment group patients were given a fixed dose of VNS for eight weeks. Anyone who has suffered chronic depression for twenty-five years, and is in a current depressive episode of 4.1 years, is not going to be cured in eight weeks. That was a completely unreasonable goal. And it contributed to the failed short- term part of the study.

O

chapter eleven

A GRADUAL RECOVERY

On Monday, February 4, 2002, I had my first visit to SLU following the negative press release discussed in Chapter Ten. The study investigators didn't mention anything about the failed acute study. I may have asked them about it, I don't remember. In any event, this visit was the standard two-hour appointment, and nothing deviated from any of the previous visits.

I assume the executives at Cyberonics were doing everything they could to salvage the study and not have to do a complete new study. And, to their credit, they found a way. Because neurological devices are considered permanent, the long-term results are considered to be much more important than the short-term results. If a drug fails the acute portion of a study, it is sent back to the research lab or completely abandoned. Since the short-term study failed because a significant number of patients in the treatment group didn't get an efficacious dose of vagus nerve stimulation, the answer was quite simple: turn up all the patients to an effective level of stimulation.

At some point during late winter of 2002, I can imagine the

chief executive officer of Cyberonics, Robert "Skip" Cummins, running out of his office and giving the order to turn everybody (the patients) up. Remember the famous scene from the *I Love Lucy Show*, where Lucy and Ethel take a job at a candy factory? The female foreman comes into the room where Lucy and Ethel are working behind a slow moving conveyer belt and she loudly shouts, "Speed it up!" That's probably a good analogy to what was going on at Cyberonics.

My next scheduled visit at SLU was Wednesday, March 6, 2002. Although I was never told I was going to have the level of stimulation increased, there's no doubt in my mind I left SLU that day at a higher setting than when I arrived. The only side effect I felt from the higher setting was a small tickle in my throat and a slight increase in hoarseness when the stimulator switched on. It was minor and easily tolerated. (I should point out that for the past year and a half I haven't felt a thing when the stimulator is activated. Virtually all of the hoarseness has disappeared.)

Thursday, March 7, 2002, was my next scheduled visit with my psychiatrist. I reiterated to the doctor that I lived a quiet life, which was okay with me. Okay is a relative term. "Normal" people would be completely unsatisfied with my "okay" life. But they have never lived in chronic mental anguish. I told the doctor there was a small uptick in my mood. This was a positive and I would take anything I could get. I still lived an isolated life, completely devoid of any social activity.

I started to be concerned about how I could make a living, while still satisfying my need to be isolated. My IRA wasn't increasing in value and a comfortable retirement sitting on the beach was not in the cards. I certainly couldn't be the outgoing salesperson I had been in my prior life. It was impossible. I didn't like to leave my home, let alone make sales calls. I was also apprehensive about falling behind in my computer skills. The whole world was changing, while I remained secluded in my condominium.

I developed an interest in the amazing concept of eBay. The fact I developed an interest in anything was remarkable. In the spring of 2002 I taught myself how to sell on eBay, then took a terrific on-line course to learn more (http://www.Vagus NerveStimulator.com/eBayCourse). I attended the very first eBay Live in June 2002 in Anaheim, California. It was great to attend the eBay Conference with five thousand other people and be totally anonymous. It was emancipating. I could relax among strangers. I was able to observe firsthand that eBay was a first-class organization and not a giant flea market.

My family, however, was appalled at my involvement in eBay. Even though I never made a lot of money selling on eBay, the experience was priceless. It jump-started me into doing something productive. And most importantly, it was clear the benefits of continuous vagus nerve stimulation were gradually "kicking in."

The very first item I ever sold on eBay was an unopened box of Anthony Robbins' *Personal Power II*, complete with 25 CDs plus videotapes. My brother, in a well-meaning gesture, suggested I purchase this self-help product that "would unleash the power within." Unfortunately, *Personal Power II* doesn't increase the flow of serotonin and norepinephrine to the brain. Anyway, I put it up for auction, it received 24 bids and sold for $240. I was so excited!

And, ultimately, eBay's tremendous success would prove my family wrong. eBay now has a market value in excess of $50 billion and, with its 140 million registered users; eBay would rank as the ninth most populous nation in the world! eBay has empowered millions of people to pursue their dreams of economic and entrepreneurial success.

Over 450,000 people make selling on the site their full-time job. If you are unable to work in an office environment, eBay could be your solution to making a living. The company offers a supportive community environment that people who suffer from depression often lack. It also offers access to healthcare solutions to sellers who average $1,000 a month in sales.

The difficulty about a therapy that works gradually is there is no cataclysmic epiphany that can be identified as the catalyst that changed everything. I had four oars in the water: vagus nerve stimulation, antidepressants, a psychiatrist, and a psychologist. Continuous stimulation of my vagus nerve slowly but surely improved my depression. The therapy had a domino affect. The antidepressants became more effective, further improving the depression, which made the psychotherapy sessions more insight-ful, which increased my activity level. I wasn't swinging from the chandeliers at any parties, but my foot was in the water.

I think psychotherapy is beneficial. I can't imagine my recov-ery without the help from my psychologist (PhD), who was and is an amazing therapist with ESP. Incredibly accurate ESP. Within the first sixty seconds of a visit, she can accurately diagnose how well I slept the night before and how I've felt since my last visit. She evaluates the way I walk into her office, how I sit on the couch, and the way I hold my hands. She gives me a quick once-over and then focuses on my face and eyes. That's it. The remaining fifty-nine minutes of the session she continues to peel the onion back.

As my depression improved, I kept telling her I was in uncharted waters; I didn't know what or how to think about what was going on. I was extremely cautious because I felt the improve-ment in my mood was fragile. I still hadn't gotten my sea legs back. It was also not a straight-line improvement. Charted on a graph, my improvement would look more like the teeth of an upward sloping handsaw. There were setbacks and bounce backs. My psychologist helped guide me through the ever-changing developments in my depression.

I cannot understand why any patient who benefits from their treatment plan (medications, therapy, etc.) stops adhering to the plan. Patient compliance is a problem in all areas of medicine, but that was the one issue I had total control over. Taking a few pills a day is simple; it is absolutely confounding to me that 50 percent of patients stop taking their medications. I never missed an office visit or one dose of medication. Yes, I have side effects from my medications, but they are tolerable when compared to the alternative: misery. If I had a chance to get better, it required 100 percent compliance. This was not something I was going to skip, ever.

You might wonder why I needed therapy if my depression was improving. The best analogy I can make is the ads that appear in the *New York Times Magazine* for high net worth clients with a minimum account size of $25 million. There's usually a picture of a serious looking "advisor" and the text states: "Wealth carries a tremendous burden and responsibility, which requires expert advice." I read these ads and wonder who are these people burdened with $25 million and looking for help? Mental health is a priceless asset that you want to protect, especially after you've lost it and are getting it back.

I was protective of any improvement, so I maintained a

"bunker" mentality for a long time. And it was the correct thing to do. Psychotherapy helped me understand the social and psychological factors that contributed to my depression. And it also helped me figure out what kind of life I wanted to live after escaping from the black hole.

Over time, people develop ways of coping with their depression. What does one do when those coping mechanisms are no longer needed? Most people are afraid of change, even if it's a positive change. It helps to have someone guide you through this newly found territory. As you feel better, you also become more aware of the things in your life that are troublesome or that negatively affected you. Depressed people avoid conflict and withdraw from situations that involve conflict. A whole new set of skills are needed to assert yourself and find your place among the people who are close to you once the depression is over.

After a lifetime of people pleasing and making sure I kept everyone happy, I realize now that I don't have to please everybody. It's impossible to make everyone happy. I end up exhausted, chasing my tail and resentful that people are taking advantage of me. I want to be liked by everyone—now I realize that is not a mandatory, self-imposed requirement for living a normal life.

The shift out of full-time people pleaser (the "former" Charlie) to something less is a good example where a whole new set of skills are needed. I need to learn the skills that assert *my* needs, while my friends and family need to get to know and understand the "new" Charlie.

The transition is not easy for the latter group, but is very liberating for me. It's a wonderful feeling: I don't have to be loved by the whole world. That in itself is a major monkey off my back.

O

chapter twelve

Is It Over?

Nobody rings a bell when it's over, if it's over. By October 2003 I was telling my family how much I was looking forward to a great Thanksgiving since I was feeling so much better than I had for many years. Instead of dreading the holidays I was looking forward to a nice Thanksgiving dinner at a club with my immediate family.

Hold on cowboy, not so fast! Family dynamics set me way back by Thanksgiving and Christmas. The details are not important, but I was so disappointed in Thanksgiving, and deathly afraid many of my recent mental health gains had been lost forever. I was hurt and angry. What was the point of shock treatments, countless therapy sessions, thousands of pills, and vagus nerve implant surgery if one's family screws it up again? I was back in the dumper, mad as hell, and scared.

Apparently this was reflected in my visit to SLU on January 14, 2003. This was the most unusual visit I had ever had at SLU. After the routine interviews and questionnaires were finished, my last stop (as usual) was with JoAnn. She asked me something different. "Do you want me to turn up the level of stimulation?"

I was shocked, but I immediately replied, "Absolutely yes. As fast as you can." I placed the programmable wand over the stimulator and less than thirty seconds later the settings were increased. For about a minute I felt a slight tickle in my throat—and that was it. I got in my car and went home.

Over the next month or so, I was back on track again. I was relieved, but it reinforced in my mind that the boogie monster (depression) could rear its ugly head at any moment. I became even more cautious and protective, like a mother bear guarding her cubs. When you have depression, rightly or wrongly, you lose your credibility and you lose respect. And you have to fight to get it back. I fought. It can get ugly. Anyone or anything that posed a threat to me got kicked in the balls. I can practically hear my family saying, "We just don't know what to say to him, he's so sensitive." Enough said!

This is another instance when the guidance of a good therapist is critical as you recover. Everything is changing; your family relationships, friendships, outside activities, etc. There's much that needs to be managed and I looked to my psychologist to guide me through the transformation from utter despair and isolation to spreading my wings little by little.

In the Helpful Resources section of my Website, www.vagus-nerve-stimulator.com, I recommend an outstanding book, *Understanding Depression*, by J. Raymond DePaulo, Jr., MD who is the Chairman of the Department of Psychiatry at the Johns Hopkins School of Medicine. It is by far the best book about the disease of depression that is available. There's a lot of self-help junk out there. If you suffer from depression (or have a loved one who does), this book is indispensable. He best describes, in one paragraph, the next six months of my recovery.

"So why does it take so long between the time the symptoms go away and when you feel back to normal? (Some patients never completely get back to normal.) What usually happens first is you begin to look better. You are no longer "leaning into the wind"—your posture is better, you move with more agility, your skin tone and color are better, and you speak more animatedly. You begin to regain some of the vitality and energy you lost when you were depressed. Yet if you were my patient and I told you that you were looking better, you'd probably think I was out of my mind. When I was a young psychiatrist and didn't realize how differently they were seeing their situation, I would comment on how much better they looked. They insisted that I was mistaken and that I was just trying to encourage them because they knew they certainly didn't *feel* any better. They were perfectly accurate about how they felt, of course, but so was I about my observation (albeit not perfectly). That's because physical improvement regularly occurs before psychological improvement. I always tell patients, "You'll look better before you feel better." The inner symptoms of hopelessness and low self-esteem take more time to recover than vitality and physical condition. Now, I just tell my patients that I've noticed that they seem to have more energy and point out that this is usually the harbinger of things to come . . ."

J. Raymond DePaulo, Jr., MD, *Understanding Depression*

I would add to Dr. DePaulo's comments that the lagging of my "inner symptoms of hopelessness" compared to my physical condition only further contributed to the confusion my family and friends felt about me. Because I looked better, they expected more than I could deliver. We didn't need any additional confusion in this situation. I felt added pressure, until finally I took off the gloves and said that's it. I have had enough. I am going to do what my professional mental health advisors and I think is right for me. I don't care what anybody else thinks. I was dead serious and I meant it. It was incredibly emancipating and ultimately accelerated my recovery.

If I had to describe the next six months, I would say that I adopted Greyhound Bus Line's strategy—"Sit back and leave the driving to us." The device was set to deliver stimulation to the vagus nerve on a regular basis. I was clearly deriving benefits from the habitual, preset stimulation of the vagus nerve, but there was nothing for me to do as a patient. Scientists now know that vagus nerve stimulation efficacy is a function of dosage (level and frequency of stimulation) and time. Perhaps I could have asked the study investigators to increase the level of stimulation to speed things along. I don't know how to best explain this clinical trial, but it was like vagus nerve stimulation boot camp.

The investigators are wonderful people and I enjoy a great relationship with all of them, but as a study patient I couldn't ask for anything (of course, if there were ever any problems, they were accessible 24/7). It was their study and they called the shots. The visits were routine and identical. There wasn't any two-way (between patient and investigator) stimulation strategy. When the programmable wand was placed over the stimulator I had no idea what, if anything, was taking place. By this time I had been well trained not to ask because they couldn't and wouldn't answer.

Mentally, things were improving; but physically I had deteriorated. I had developed a herniated disc and gained thirty-three pounds, as well as four-and-a-half inches around my waist. I was in chronic excruciating pain. Greyhound Bus strategy would not help my physical condition. But eventually I had the motivation, drive, and more importantly had lost the fear (agoraphobia), so I could go to the gym and exercise. I lost the weight between February and August of 2003, but I was not getting significant pain relief. I had to take pain pills on a daily basis. I tried everything to relieve the pain; physical therapy twice a week, physical therapy exercises five to six days a week, weekly sixty-minute back massages, Eastern acupuncture, chiropractors, and pain specialists. I considered going to an Islamic religious healer. I did go to a sacro-cranial massage therapist—the treatment was part massage and part psychotherapy. After our first ninety-minute session, she told me that the cause of my pain was my inner child crying in my sacrum. (Oh, really? Well, that may be true, but I'm getting out of here! I want pain relief. My inner child will just have to wait.) I tried everything I could think of because back surgery was absolutely the last option.

In the end I was swimming three or four days a week, had private pilates sessions two days a week, and had thirty minutes of pelvic/lower back traction four times a week. There was still no significant relief from the pain. Finally, I was referred to an incredible medical doctor who specialized in pain resulting from injuries. She was much more than just an expert in pain; she was also a board certified anesthesiologist with special accredited training in rehabilitation in the treatment of injuries and pain. Her approach to pain relief was unlike any I had ever seen before. She focused on the integration of the physical anatomy, injury physiology, physical and structural changes, and their effects on pain. She worked side-by-side with a highly skilled physical therapist. I walked into the exam room and told her that I had tried absolutely everything, and had even lost thirty-three pounds. She said she hated me (jokingly), and then the doctor and her physical therapist did the most thorough, most unusual, and most complete physical exam I had ever had.

After the exam she said two things that shocked me. First she said my body felt like it had rigor mortis and second she was positive she could help me. Rigor mortis? I had felt mentally dead, but my body was still functioning, and I was very active physically. She told me I was as tight as a drum, and there were parts of my body that weren't moving at all. That meant the rest of my body had to compensate, and that was what was causing the pain.

Moshe Feldenkrais, author of the books *Functional Integration* and *Awareness through Movement* best describes my condition in his books when he says the body carries with it all of life's experiences, good and bad. My body carried a whole lot from the years of depression. I had a series of trigger point injections (over three months) that were strategically given in various muscles of my body. The injections caused the tight muscles to spasm and release. I felt pain relief within twenty-four hours of each injection. It was another life-altering event in a life full of altering events.

Dr. John Sarno of NYU's Medical Center Rusk Institute of Rehabilitation did a study several years ago of ninety patients suffering from back pain. He discovered that depression was the cause of the pain in almost half the patients. The cover of the April 26, 2004 issue of *Newsweek* magazine featured a story titled "Treating Back Pain." Although the article was about the 65 million Americans with back pain, there were at least fifteen references to an emotional or mental health issue (depression, anxiety, etc.). The problem of co-morbidity is just beginning to be studied and will hopefully be a catalyst for treating the mental health of the patient, which will help with many of the patient's other healthcare issues. The total cost of back pain in the United States is estimated to be $100 billion annually and the cost of depression is estimated at $80 billion.

I still do pilates, physical therapy, and swimming on a weekly basis, and there are parts of my body that are moving for the first time in many years. The mental illness of depression literally destroyed my physical body. Every time I forced myself to do what other people wanted me to do, my body tightened up. The tight muscles did not get enough blood, so the muscles did not get the oxygen they needed. Over many years I had done count-less things that other people thought were good for me, and I paid a physical price. The great news is that the physical pain is steadily getting less, but if I slack off for a week or two the pain returns. I am fully committed to maintaining the physical part of my recov-ery. The mental and physical problems are related; the physical damage resulted from a long life of mental illness (depression).

The American Psychiatric Association explains the relation-ship between depression and physical symptoms. Please see Appendix F for the article about this topic, which is reprinted with permission from Medscape.

chapter thirteen

FIRST YOU HUM TO THE MUSIC

My depression and mood continued to improve for the remainder of the year. Researchers now know that mood and depression can continue to improve for up to two years AFTER the patient has been ramped up to an efficacious dose of stimulation. I still wake up every morning asking myself, "Is it (the depression) back?" By the time I get in the shower the answer is the same: no. I am much less suspicious of the improvement in my depression now than I was a year ago. I used to drive by myself in a car for hours, in dead silence. Now, I drive with the radio blaring or with a CD playing, singing to the music and moving to the beat.

At one point during the recovery process, I told my psychologist if you could out a ribbon and put it around the way I feel, I'd take it. It was like letting the air out of a balloon that was about to pop. It only took a relatively modest improvement in my mood to provide some relief from the mental oppression that I had suffered from for so many years. However, if I had taken that deal, it would have been a mistake. My mood and depression continued to steadily improve.

Because my mood improvement was gradual there was no epiphany, the most remarkable thing about this treatment is the staying power of the therapy. It's like the Energizer™ bunny; it keeps on going and going. Things keep getting better and better. Any sadness I experience is a normal emotion that anyone would have in response to a negative event. But unlike when I was in the throes of depression, my mood eventually brightens to a normal level.

My wobbly sea legs have gotten stronger and I have become more and more confident. I am not afraid to go to a shopping mall, nor do I have to race through the aisles of the grocery store. Last weekend I attended a small dinner party hosted by someone I had not seen or talked to in over five years. A year ago I never would have considered attending, but then again, I wouldn't have been invited. The friends I lost touch with would have been uncertain about me and whether a dinner invitation would have been appropriate. I ran into this friend at a wake and I assume he could see from the way I acted that I had regained much of my confidence and swagger back. I think it gave him the assurance that it was okay to invite me to his dinner party.

I am also more engaged in life. I hired a Webmaster to help me start a Website, VagusNerveStimulator.com, which was launched in February 2004. Finding a Webmaster to create a mental health Website was an interesting process since nobody wanted to have anything to do with creating a mental health Website. My idea sounded crazy. Porn, gambling, or a site promoting illegal drugs from overseas would have been easier to start than a site on mental illness.

One Webmaster I contacted wanted to name the site "cure-my-depression-now.com." Can you imagine anyone recommending a similar name for a physical illness? How about "cure-my-cancer-now.com?" While a name like that would be considered inhumane for a physical illness, the same standard does not apply to mental illnesses. It's not fair, but it is life.

Finally, I discovered a wonderful Webmaster from Montreal, Marc Deschamps. He has been with me from the beginning. He is ethical, loyal and has taken a personal interest in the success of the site and newsletter.

I wanted my Website to be an information source for sufferers of chronic or treatment-resistant depression. We used a simple, inexpensive all-in-one, site-building product (http://www.sitesell.com/buildaweb.html). The very first month, the VagusNerve Stimulator.com site received over 8,000 visitors. I was shocked. But for the first time, it verified to me that there were many people searching for a solution to the debilitating disease of depression. I was not alone.

All of the articles are written by mental health professionals and nationally recognized mental health organizations. I am pleased with the high quality of the content. I also wanted the site to be an introduction to vagus nerve stimulation since it is a potential breakthrough medical device for the treatment of chronic depression. Although the outcome and timing of the FDA's approval was uncertain, vagus nerve stimulation sounded like voodoo medicine and it needed to be demystified.

I decided to write this book about my personal battle with depression, my participation in the investigational clinical trial, and the miraculous rebound in my depression due to the stimulator. I hope my story helps you. I am absolutely overwhelmed with gratitude by the powerful recovery that I have experienced. I thought I was a goner, with the next forty-five years of my life stuck in utter despair.

There has been an almost complete turnaround in my life. Right now I am "integrating"—that's the term mental health professionals use to describe this part of my recovery. When someone has been acutely ill for such a long time, every part of the recovery takes longer, including integrating. I had a huge chunk taken out of my life. I lost a lot of time. I am so humbled by the joy and happiness I am now able to experience. I don't have to keep up appearances any more. I love looking at the blooming dogwood trees, colorful azaleas, and smelling the fresh spring air. The Fourth of July is no longer the harbinger of doom and gloom and the upcoming holiday season. If you could package the way I feel now and put a ribbon around it, I'd take it. I don't want or need anything more. If you have your health (physical and mental), a good family, a couple of close friends, and food on the table, you have everything. (Well almost everything—it's time that I restart building that "IRA" thing.)

Thank you for reading my story. The remainder of the book includes technical information, reprinted articles by pyschiatric thought leaders, FDA's approval letter, as well as additional personal commentary by me.

Ultimately, you must follow the advice and directives of your doctor. However, in my opinion, if you suffer from treatment-resistant chronic depression, the VNS Therapy™ should be strongly considered as a therapeutic option.

I wish you the best of luck. May you be as lucky as me.

O

chapter fourteen

ABOUT CYBERONICS, INC.

I have been asked many times how I ever thought
of this idea or if I made the device in my garage or basement. I
don't even own a Phillip's head screwdriver, so it would have been
highly unlikely that I invented the vagus nerve stimulator. No, the
device was developed and is manufactured by a publicly held
medical device company, Cyberonics, Inc.

Cyberonics is not a start-up company; it has been in business
since 1987 and has spent over $150,000,000 to research and
develop just one product: the VNS Therapy System™.
Cyberonics is profitable and has over $100 million in cash on its
balance sheet and a market value of over $850,000,000.

In August 2005, Cyberonics announced that Vagus Nerve
Stimulation (VNS) Therapy has accumulated more than 100,000
patient years of experience, making it the most widely used neurostimulation device for the treatment of epilepsy, depression, and
central nervous system (CNS) disorders. Eight years after FDA
approval as an adjunctive therapy used to reduce the frequency
of seizures in adults and adolescents over twelve years of age

with partial onset seizures that are refractory to antiepileptic medications, VNS Therapy has been used to treat more than 32,000 patients worldwide. The VNS Therapy System™ is now considered a mainstream treatment for pharmaco-resistant epilepsy.

In the investigational trials for epilepsy in the mid-1990s, the study investigators noticed many of the patients were reporting an improvement in mood. This unintended benefit was the catalyst for a small pilot study (59 patients) to further investigate vagus nerve stimulation for people suffering from depression. Based on the encouraging results from the pilot study, Cyberonics took the next step and designed the FDA-approved protocol for a 235-patient, double-blind, placebo-controlled study.

Cyberonics' largest shareholder is Boston Scientific Corporation, a medical device company with over $4 billion in annual sales. Boston Scientifics' purchase of approximately 14.9 percent of Cyberonics is recognition of the value of Cyberonics' VNS Therapy System™, intellectual property, epilepsy, and depression businesses. In March 2005, *Business Week Magazine* recognized Cyberonics as the leading company in the field of neuromodulation. It is safe to say that I didn't make the stimulator in my garage.

Cyberonics now employs over 500 people. Its European subsidiary (Cyberonics Europe S.A.) is based in Belgium. In addition to Canada, the company has medical consultants in Germany, France, Belgium, and the United Kingdom marketing the VNS Therapy System. Cyberonics is headquartered in Houston, Texas:

Cyberonics, Inc., The Cyberonics Building
100 Cyberonics Boulevard
Houston, Texas 77058
Telephone: 1 (877) NOW-4VNS or 1-877-869-4867

If you are interested in considering VNS Therapy™ as a treatment option, I would encourage you to call the telephone number listed in the above paragraph and ask to speak with a Case Manager responsible for your geographic area. The Case Managers are highly trained, HIPAA compliant, clinical nurses. The Case Manager is essentially your "go to" person for further patient education, insurance reimbursement issues, as well as referrals to psychiatrists and/or surgeons near you trained in vagus nerve stimulation therapy.

There are many other resources available to you on the Cyberonics' Website, www.vnstherapy.com as well as additional patient information on my Website, www.VagusNerveStimulator. com

Full disclosure: I am not a shareholder of Cyberonics.

chapter fifteen

WHAT IS VAGUS NERVE STIMULATION?

Vagus Nerve Stimulation (VNS) is not brain surgery, although it is a treatment that affects the function of the brain. Vagus nerve stimulation uses specific stimulation of the vagus nerve to send stimulation to specific parts of the brain that are involved in mood. It is not like Electro-Convulsive Therapy (ECT), a treatment that involves stimulation of the entire brain and induces convulsions in patients.

In fact, patients may not even feel the stimulation from VNS since the vagus nerve does not have the types of nerves that carry pain signals. Nor does VNS interfere with drugs, thus patients having VNS therapy can continue taking their medications without worrying about side effects or interactions between drugs.

What is the vagus nerve?

Vagus means "wandering" in Latin, and is the perfect description for the vagus nerve, the longest nerve in the body. It averages almost two feet in length and "wanders" throughout the upper body. The vagus nerve starts in the brain, goes down the neck, and into the body where it affects the vocal cords, the acid content of the stomach, the heart, the lungs, and other organs. In the brain it projects to areas believed to be responsible for seizures, mood, appetite, memory, and anxiety.[1] However, the vagus nerve cord does not have many pain nerves, so stimulation of the vagus nerve is not painful, although some patients may feel some sensation when electrical pulses are generated.

The history of vagus nerve stimulation

Vagus nerve stimulation has been used to treat epilepsy patients for years; the first human clinical trial was in 1988,[2] and the FDA approved VNS therapy for epilepsy in 1997.[3] So far over 30,000 people worldwide have had VNS therapy, and it has proven to be a safe and effective treatment for epilepsy.[4] These patients have reported minimal side effects, which have tended to decrease over time. The efficacy of the treatment has also been shown to increase with longer treatment time.[5]

When Vagus Nerve Stimulation was first approved for epilepsy, some patients reported an improvement in mood. Researchers decided to design a study specifically to measure changes in a patient's mood and depression due to stimulation of the vagus nerve. In 1999, scientists began the first open label (no placebo group) study for depression with 60 patients. This first study found that there was indeed an improvement in mood for de-pressed patients. Based on this study, a more detailed and thorough study was designed to determine if vagus nerve stimulation would be a safe, tolerable, and effective treatment for chronic depression.

The completed one-year, double-blind, placebo controlled trial had 235 patients from twenty-one participating hospitals in the United States, and showed clinically significant improvements due to treatment compared to baseline.[6] The acute (short-term) phase lasted three months, during which half of the patients received stimulation (treatment group) and half did not (control group). The long-term phase of the study lasted an additional three years of stimulation. The HRSD-24 (24 item clinician-rated Hamilton Rating Scale for Depression) improvements observed over the first year were highly significant. The results of this long-term, pivotal study were submitted to the FDA in October 2003; the FDA's Medical Devices Advisory Panel recommended approval of VNS for chronic depression on June 15, 2004. Final FDA approval was issued on July 8, 2005. Of note, Vagus Nerve Stimulation therapy was approved for use in patients with treatment-resistant depression in the European Union in March 2001, and in Canada in April 2001.[7]

How does VNS therapy work?

The Pulse Generator (battery) delivers a small amount of electrical current to the vagus nerve intermittently (thirty seconds on and five minutes off) twenty-four hours a day, seven days a week for up to ten years.[8] The stimulation is delivered automatically, so the patient does not have to do anything. Because there is nothing to remember, compliance is assured. The stimulation is not supposed to be uncomfortable; some patients do not even feel it. A nurse at the doctor's office can adjust the level of stimulation (amount of electricity delivered) if the patient ever feels uncomfortable. In the study reviewed by the FDA, researchers noted several similarities between epileptic and depressed patients.[9]

One of the most important similarities is that VNS treatment efficacy improves *over time*. The *longer* the patient receives stimulation, the *better* the results. In addition, both populations of patients share the following:

- Assured adherence to treatment regimen
- Safety of the procedure
- Safety of the therapy
- High continuation rates

- No drug interactions
- No cognitive impairment (memory loss)

What is the surgery like?

Vagus nerve stimulation is NOT brain surgery, even though it is an invasive surgical procedure that changes the function of the brain. The stimulator is a pacemaker-like device that generates electrical pulses (Pulse Generator); it is implanted under the skin in the left chest through a small incision. While this may sound like a dangerous procedure, it is not. The FDA has approved the use and confirmed the safety of this procedure. More than 30,000 patients have received the implant to treat epilepsy. The vagus nerve stimulation surgery involves two small incisions, one in the chest and one at the lowest part of the neck. At no time does the surgeon physically manipulate the brain.

The surgery to implant the VNS System takes forty-five minutes to two hours. Local, regional, or general anesthesia (putting the patient to sleep) is used during the surgery; the doctor and anesthetist determine which type of anesthesia is best for each patient. Most VNS patients will have outpatient surgery, but some patients may need to stay in the hospital overnight, and in that case they will need a family member or companion to take them home from the hospital.[10]

What happens after the VNS surgery?

Most VNS patients go home the same day or the next day. You will feel some minor stiffness/soreness around the area of the implant for a few days. Your doctor may prescribe a minor pain medication such as Tylenol™ with codeine. A week later your surgeon will probably want to check the scars and a nurse can program/change the settings on the stimulator in the doctor's office.

What are the most common side effects?

Hoarseness is the most common side effect from the stimulation, which is what I experienced. Over time, my hoarseness dissipated and is now virtually unnoticeable. Patient experience indicates that, as a rule, side effects become less noticeable over time and typically do not result in patients discontinuing the therapy.

Obviously if it is determined that you ultimately are deriving no benefit from the stimulation, the Pulse Generator can be turned off. If you are benefiting from stimulation, however, the side effects are minor and tolerable. Any improvement in your depression can be life-changing.

According to Cyberonics' presentation to the FDA Panel on June 15, 2004, the most common side effects reported after the first year of stimulation are:

Voice alteration	56%
Increased cough	6%
Shortness of breath	16%
Neck pain	13%
Sore throat	5%
Tingling	4%
Nausea	2%
Incision pain	6%

Is the VNS surgery final?

The vagus nerve stimulator can be turned off or removed (explanted) at any time if the patient feels it is not helping, or in the unlikely event the patient can't tolerate the stimulation. The device can be completely turned off in less than thirty seconds in the doctor's office. All it requires is for a nurse to hold a programmable wand over the skin above the Pulse Generator.

Explantation (removal) of the vagus nerve stimulation device is possible. Just like implantation, the surgery to remove the

The Cyberonics Magnet can be used to stop the stimulation.
This particular model can clip onto your belt.

device is a simple procedure. Only the Pulse Generator is taken
out of the body; attempting to remove the electrode from around
the vagus nerve could cause damage, and is not recommended.

The Cyberonics Magnet

Cyberonics will provide you with the Magnet before the
implant procedure At any time, you can stop the stimulation with
the Cyberonics Magnet. The Magnet can be used to stop the
stimulation temporarily or to turn off the Generator. I never had
to use the Magnet and my understanding is that few patients
needed the Magnet. But, if you plan to sing or speak publicly and

if the stimulation bothers you, the Magnet may be useful to you. You simply place the Magnet over the area of the Pulse Generator, and the stimulation will be stopped. When the Magnet is removed, the VNS Therapy System™ is turned back on.

Notes

1. Vagus Nerve Stimulation Therapy Mechanisms of Action. September 24, 2003 presentation by M.S. George, MD. Medical University of South Carolina, Charleston, SC, USA.

2. Pharmacoresistant Epilepsy and VNS Therapy. September 24, 2003 presentation by J.W. Wheless, MD. The University of Texas Health Science Center, Houston TX, USA.

3. Form 10-Q for Cyberonics Inc, September 4, 2003.

4. Vagus Nerve Stimulation Therapy Mechanisms of Action. September 24, 2003 presentation by M.S. George, MD. Medical University of South Carolina, Charleston, SC, USA.

5. Form 10-Q for Cyberonics Inc, September 4, 2003.

6.Ibid.

7.Ibid.

8. Vagus Nerve Stimulation Therapy Mechanisms of Action. September 24, 2003 presentation by M.S. George, MD. Medical University of South Carolina, Charleston, SC, USA.

9. The Investigation of Vagus Nerve Stimulation Therapy in Treatment-Resistant Depression. September 24, 2003 presentation by R.L. Rudolph, MD. Cyberonics, Inc.

6. Vagus Nerve Stimulation Therapy Mechanisms of Action. September 24, 2003 presentation by M.S. George, MD. Medical University of South Carolina, Charleston, SC, USA.

O

chapter sixteen

THE IMPLANT PROCEDURE

The information on the implant procedure may
sound intricate and might unfairly cloud the procedure as a dangerous operation. As you read this information, realize that
medical device chest implants have been done since 1958 and the
operation has been safely performed on more than 30,000
epilepsy patients.

Note: You need to rely upon the experts (neurosurgeons, vascular surgeons, and ENTs) to assess the risk of implanting the
VNS Therapy System.

The VNS Therapy System™ consists of the VNS Therapy
Pulse Generator, the Bipolar Lead, the programming wand and
software, and the tunneling tool. The VNS Pulse Generator (the
vagus nerve stimulator) and Bipolar Lead are surgically implanted
while the patient is under general, regional, or local anesthesia.
The VNS Pulse Generator is surgically implanted in a subcutaneous pocket in the upper left chest. The Bipolar Lead is
connected to the VNS Pulse Generator and attached to the vagus

nerve in the lower left side of the patient's neck. The patient is generally admitted to the hospital the day of surgery and discharged the same or the following day.

How does the VNS therapy work?

The VNS Therapy System™ delivers vagus nerve stimulation therapy on a continual intermittent basis. The initial standard stimulation parameters that are recommended by Cyberonics, are a thirty-second period of stimulation, which they refer to as ON time, followed by a five-minute period without stimulation, which is referred to as OFF time. To optimize patient treatment, the pulse width, output current, signal frequency, stimulation duration, and stimulation OFF intervals of the VNS Pulse Generator can be non-invasively programmed and adjusted by the treating physician with a personal computer using Cyberonics' programming wand and software. In addition, the patient can use a small, hand-held magnet that is provided with the VNS Pulse Generator to manually activate or deactivate stimulation. The magnet can also be used to provide patient control of stimulation side effects by allowing the patient to temporarily deactivate the Pulse Generator.

No one knows exactly why stimulation to the vagus nerve works. But in the various clinical trials, continuous stimulation to the vagus nerve has been shown to favorably modulate those areas of the brain that are responsible for regulating mood and depression.

The VNS Pulse Generator

The Pulse Generator of the VNS Therapy System™ is an implantable, programmable, cardiac pacemaker-like signal generator designed to be coupled with the bipolar lead to deliver electrical signals to the vagus nerve. The VNS Pulse Generator (vagus nerve stimulator) employs a battery that has an expected life of approximately five to eight years at standard stimulation

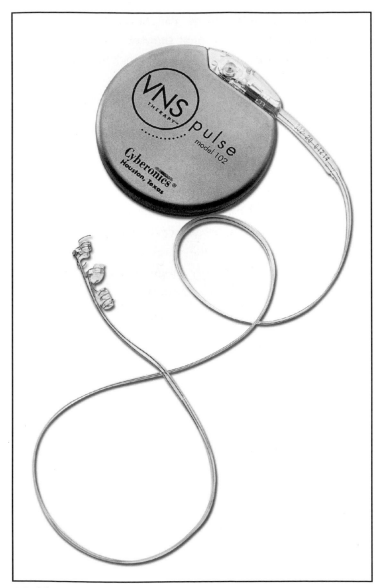

Model 102 Pulse Generator.

parameters. Upon expiration of the battery, the VNS Pulse Generator is removed and a new generator is implanted in a short, outpatient procedure using local anesthesia. Replacement of the lead is a different procedure. It is rarely done and is not required for routine replacement of the Pulse Generator.

Stimulator Statistics

The actual Model 102 VNS Therapy Generator is about the size of a pocket watch. It weighs less than an ounce. Cyberonics plans to introduce the Model 103 NCP Pulse Generator in 2005. The newer model will be smaller than the one currently available, the Model 102. Here are some of the statistics for the Model 102:

Weight: 8/10 of an ounce
Diameter: 2.0 inches
Thinness: ¼ of an inch thin
Battery Life: 6-11 years (Battery life is dependent on the stimulation parameters determined by your physician.)

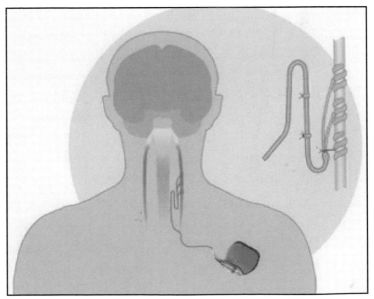

Location of the implant.

Bipolar Lead

Cyberonics has licensed a proprietary nerve lead to convey the electrical signal from the VNS Pulse Generator to the vagus nerve. The lead incorporates patented electrodes that are self-sizing and flexible, minimizing mechanical trauma to the nerve and allowing body fluid interchange within the nerve structure. The lead's electrode and anchor tether wrap around the vagus nerve and the connector end is tunneled subcutaneously to the chest where it is attached to the VNS Pulse Generator. The lead for the VNS Therapy is available in two sizes of inner spiral diameter to ensure optimal electrode placement on different sized nerves.

Programming wand and software

The VNS Therapy System™ includes a proprietary programming wand and software, used to interrogate the device and to transmit programming information from a personal computer to the VNS Pulse Generator via electromagnetic signals. These products are compatible with both Pentium and non-Pentium-based platform personal computers. Programming capabilities include modification of the VNS Pulse Generator's programmable parameters (pulse width, output current, signal frequency, and stimulation duration and interval) and storage and retrieval of telemetry data. The VNS Therapy programming wand can be connected to a standard personal computer using a serial connector.

There are many variables that can influence the outcome of VNS therapy and they are different for each patient:

- ON/OFF Cycle: The time interval between periods of stimulation.
- Pulse Width: The duration of a single pulse within a period of stimulation. This is measured in microseconds.
- Stimulation Frequency: The number of single pulses of stimulation delivered per second, expressed in hertz.

Tunneling tool

The tunneling tool is a single-use sterile, disposable surgical tool designed to be used during surgical placement of the Bipolar Lead. This VNS Therapy tool is used for subcutaneous tunneling of the lead assembly between the nerve site in the neck and the VNS Pulse Generator site in the chest.

Notes

Source: SEC Form 10-K, Cyberonics,Inc.—July 2003.

O
chapter seventeen

SHOULD YOU CONSIDER VNS?

Let me borrow a quote from Dr. Phil: "If you have been going to the same problem solver for ten years and you ain't gettin' any better, then you need to find a new problem solver." Change "problem solver" to antidepressants and add a Texas twang to the quote, and this may steer you to try an alternative treatment. Maybe it's vagus nerve stimulation, maybe not. But, if you are living your life with chronic depression, then something has to change.

Because the VNS Therapy System™ is not something you can purchase at your local drugstore, you will receive plenty of advice and guidance from your doctors regarding the implant procedure and your post-operation activities. For me, once I was 100 percent comfortable that the procedure was safe, there was nothing else to think about. My analysis was like the Nike commercial: "Just Do It". My family's scrutiny consisted of: "When the hell are you going to do it?!"

In life, we don't get to choose the diseases we suffer from, nor do we get to choose the potential remedy for the disease. For chronic, treatment-resistant depression, VNS Therapy is the mainstream treatment for patients who are experiencing a major depressive episode and have not adequately responded to traditional antidepressants. Rather than be intimidated by the procedure, applaud yourself for considering the most aggressive, leading-edge treatment for the biological disease of depression.

Now that I have the implant, I think there are times when my family would like to have my stimulation settings turned down!

Unlike the closely guarded secret of my shock treatments, I was much more open with friends and relatives about the vagus nerve stimulation procedure to help my depression. There is a terrible stigma associated with electroconvulsive therapy. In contrast, I didn't feel shame or embarrassment about vagus nerve stimulation. The VNS Therapy System™ is a more conventional, physical remedy to a mental health disease. Shock treatments will never be considered conventional.

With depression, sometimes the goal of treatment is to make a *very* depressed patient *less* depressed. If you have been suffering from chronic depression for a long time, a twenty or thirty percent improvement in mood can make a significant difference in the quality of your life. If I asked the 4.5 million people who suffer from the disabling disease of chronic depression, if they would take a 30 percent improvement in the quality of their day-to-day lives, I am confident every one of them would say yes.

As with any medical procedure, the common-sense advice is to temper your expectations for the outcome. It should be clear to you by now that VNS Therapy works slowly and gradually. This is not an operation where the surgeon comes out of the oper-

ating room and tells your family, "We got it (the disease) all out."
It can take months for the benefits to kick in. Some patients continue to derive benefit from the pre-set continuous stimulation of
the vagus nerve for up to two years after the implant. Likewise, it
can take over a year before it is finally determined that VNS
Therapy is not helping your depression. There is still so much to
be learned about the power of this therapy and the stimulation
settings that produce the optimal response in each patient.

Your decision comes down to a risk/benefit analysis. VNS
Therapy is safe. That's not my opinion, it's documented by Cyberonics' epilepsy patient registry. VNS Therapy is not a cure for
depression. However, in the clinical trials in which VNS Therapy
was used as an adjunctive long-term treatment for chronic depression, over half of the patients achieved an Extraordinary, Highly
Meaningful or Meaningful clinical benefit after twelve months of
VNS.[1]

Benefits of Vagus Nerve Stimulation (VNS)

- VNS is more effective than antidepressants for TRD
- No cognitive impairment (i.e., no memory loss)
- VNS does not have the side effects of antidepressants
- Once the device is activated, there's no further action required. Compliance is guaranteed.
- Efficacy improves over time (No "Prozac™ poop out")
- Quality-of-life benefits improve over time
- No drug interactions
- VNS is not related to brain surgery

After the implant, life goes on. You continue to stick strictly to
the treatment plan prescribed by your doctor. Take all of your pre-

scribed medications; continue with psychotherapy and or a support group, take good care of yourself, and only do things you feel comfortable doing.

Both the success and failure of VNS Therapy bring their own set of challenges for the patient. You need to have your team in place to help guide you through this process. My psychologist and psychiatrist were invaluable in monitoring my progress (or lack thereof) and made adjustments as necessary.

Notes

1. Cyberonics presentation to FDA Advisory Panel—June 15, 2004.

O

chapter eighteen

DEPRESSION PATIENT'S MANUAL

I am including a portion of the manual in this book to give you a quick reference about VNS Therapy™ for depression. This will be helpful as you begin to consider this procedure. Initially it may seem like a lot of information to understand. I know from personal experience that it can be very difficult to concentrate or remember information when you are suffering from depression. This will give you a head start, so you won't feel overwhelmed.

You will be given the entire *Depression Patient's Manual* by your doctor or the Cyberonics' Case Manager who is assigned to you. The *Depression Patient's Manual* has been reviewed by the FDA and is posted on the FDA's Website. This ensures that you get the most accurate and thoroughly reviewed information by medical experts. The excerpts included in this chapter are directly from the FDA's Website, so the reprint material looks different from the text of this book.

Ultimately, you must follow the directives of your doctor. But this should provide a solid, authoritative background for discussion with your doctor. It is not meant to replace the advice of your doctor. As a study subject, I had very little background data. This was truly a pioneering study. I don't know whether it is easier to have too much or too little information. I had only one major concern: Was this a safe procedure? The answer was emphatically yes! After that answer, I had nothing to lose.

1. INTRODUCTION TO VNS THERAPY

Many people have depression. Through the years, doctors and scientists have learned much about depression. They have developed drugs and other treatments. Despite these efforts, some people still have depression. Your doctor has proposed the VNS Therapy™ System for you to reduce the symptoms of your depression because drugs have failed to control them adequately.

The VNS Therapy System sends a mild electrical impulse to a nerve that goes to the brain. This nerve is called the vagus nerve. The treatment is Vagus Nerve Stimulation (VNS) Therapy (VNS Therapy™).

2. THE VNS THERAPY SYSTEM

2.1. Parts of the VNS Therapy System

The VNS System has several implantable and nonimplantable parts (see Figure 1 and Figure 2).

2.1.1. Implantable parts

♦ VNS Therapy Pulse Generator

♦ VNS Therapy Lead

Figure 1. Implantable parts of the VNS Therapy System

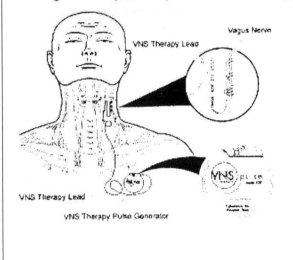

Patient/Depression-2

2.1.2. Nonimplantable parts

♦ VNS Therapy Computer

♦ VNS Therapy Programming Software

♦ VNS Therapy Programming Wand

♦ VNS Therapy Magnets

Figure 2. Nonimplantable parts of the VNS Therapy System

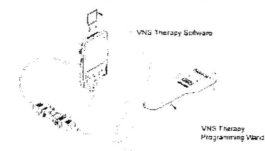

2.1.3. Pulse Generator

The main part is the Pulse Generator, sometimes called a stimulator. Similar to cardiac pacemakers, which have been used since 1958 to control heart problems, the Pulse Generator is computer controlled and battery powered. It sends signals through the electrodes of the Lead to the brain by way of the left vagus nerve.

2.1.4. Placement of the Pulse Generator and Lead

The Pulse Generator is placed under the skin of the upper chest. The Lead connects the Pulse Generator to the vagus nerve. It is surgically attached to the left vagus nerve in the neck. A surgeon implants the Pulse Generator and Lead during an operation that typically lasts about 1 to 2 hours. Later, your doctor sets the Pulse Generator to deliver periodic stimulation 24 hours a day (for example, 30 minutes ON and 5 minutes OFF). At the office, your doctor can read and change stimulation settings with the Computer, Software, and Programming Wand.

2.1.5. Cyberonics Magnet

Cyberonics provides a Magnet for you to stop stimulation if and when you need to (see the "Using Your Cyberonics Magnets" section of this manual).

2.1.6. Stimulation settings

The Pulse Generator has many settings. Your doctor will choose the settings. He or she can change (reprogram) the periodic stimulation at any time with the Programming Wand, Software, and Computer. Most of the time, changing the VNS Therapy System settings is a painless procedure, takes only a few minutes, and can be done in the doctor's office.

2.1.7. Pulse Generator life

The battery in the Pulse Generator can last from 1 to 16 years.

The lifespan depends on these factors:

♦   Pulse Generator model

- Settings your doctor chooses

- Interaction of the Lead and vagus nerve over time

When the battery in your Pulse Generator runs out, the Pulse Generator must be replaced in order for you to continue to receive VNS Therapy. This requires an additional surgical procedure. The operation involves anesthesia and generally takes less than an hour to complete. Please refer to the "Battery depletion (running out)" section of this manual for additional information about battery depletion.

3. QUICK REFERENCE GUIDE

This quick guide provides important information about the VNS Therapy System. It will be most useful after you have read the whole manual. A list of frequently asked questions is included at the end of this manual.

When you see this symbol ⚠, pay special attention to the important information after it.

After you receive your VNS Therapy System, keep this important information in mind.

- You should not receive a VNS Therapy System implant if your left vagus nerve has previously been cut.

- You CANNOT have any short-wave diathermy, microwave diathermy, or therapeutic ultrasound diathermy anywhere on your body if you have an implanted VNS Therapy System.

- **Use the Cyberonics Magnet to stop the stimulation** if it becomes painful or irregular (see the "Using Your Cyberonics Magnets" section of this manual).

- **Call your doctor right away** if any of the following occur:

  - Your voice is constantly hoarse.

  - Stimulation becomes painful or irregular.

  - Stimulation causes any choking, trouble with breathing, trouble with swallowing, or change in heart rate.

  - You or someone else notices changes in your level of consciousness (for example, you become constantly drowsy).

Patient/Depression-6

♦ You think that the Pulse Generator may not be stimulating properly or that the VNS Therapy System battery is depleted (stops stimulating).

♦ You notice anything new or unusual that you relate to the stimulation.

♦ The feeling that you usually have during stimulation becomes stronger or weaker (see the "Complications" section of this manual).

♦ Your depressive symptoms increase or suicidality (suicidal thoughts or behavior) increases. See the "Additional Safety Considerations" section of this manual for details.

♦ Call your doctor before you have **any medical tests** that might affect, or be affected by, the VNS Therapy System, such as magnetic resonance imaging (MRI) scans (see the "Medical Hazards" section of this manual).

♦ Call your doctor before you have **any other medical devices implanted** (see the "Medical Hazards" section of this manual).

♦ Tell your doctor at your next visit if you no longer feel the routine stimulation. Your doctor may decide to change your settings.

Cyberonics *cannot* provide health care advice or services. Your source for health questions must always be your doctor.

4. WHO USES VNS THERAPY?

VNS Therapy has been approved for people with chronic or recurrent treatment resistant depression who have failed to respond to four or more adequate treatments. It is *not* right for everyone who has depression. You and your doctor will decide if VNS Therapy is right for you. Your doctor will also decide if you have any other medical conditions that might be affected by VNS Therapy.

4.1. Indications for Use

The VNS Therapy System is indicated for the adjunctive long-term treatment of chronic or recurrent depression for patients 18 years of age or older who are experiencing a major depressive episode and have not had an adequate response to four or more adequate antidepressant treatments.

4.2. Contraindications (When VNS Therapy Should Not Be Used)

⚠ CONTRAINDICATION: The VNS Therapy System should not be used (is contraindicated) in people who have had the left vagus nerve cut to treat another disorder (a left vagotomy).

⚠ CONTRAINDICATION: Inform anyone treating you that you CANNOT have any short-wave diathermy, microwave diathermy, or therapeutic ultrasound diathermy (hereafter referred to as "diathermy") anywhere on your body because you have an implanted VNS Therapy System (sometimes referred to as a "Vagus Nerve Stimulator" or "Vagus Nerve

Stimulation"). **Diagnostic ultrasound is not included in this contraindication.**

Diathermy is a treatment to promote healing or relieve pain. It is provided by special medical equipment (diathermy equipment) in a doctor's office, dentist's office, or other healthcare setting.

Energy from diathermy therapy may cause heating of the VNS Therapy System. The heating of the VNS Therapy System resulting from diathermy can cause temporary or permanent nerve or tissue or vascular damage. This damage may result in pain or discomfort, loss of vocal cord function, or even possibly death if there is damage to blood vessels.

Diathermy may also damage parts of your VNS Therapy System. This damage can result in loss of therapy from your VNS Therapy System. More surgery may be required to remove or replace parts of your implanted device.

Injury or damage can occur during diathermy treatment whether your VNS Therapy System is turned "ON" or "OFF."

7. BENEFITS OF VNS THERAPY

The effectiveness of VNS Therapy in decreasing depressive symptoms was primarily demonstrated by improved scores on standardized tests after 12 months and 24 months of VNS Therapy in the D-02 study. See "Overview of Clinical Studies" in the preceding section for a description of the D-02 study.

7.1.   Effectiveness Results From the D-02 Clinical Study

7.1.1.   Three-month results

At the end of the first 3 months, the proportion of patients who had at least a 50% reduction in depression symptoms was 15% in the group of patients receiving active stimulation, slightly better than for patients who were not receiving stimulation (10% of these patients had at least a 50% reduction in symptoms). (See Table 2.) This finding suggested that the full effects of VNS Therapy might require more than 3 months of treatment.

7.1.2.   One-year results

After 1 year of VNS Therapy, the results showed that 30% of the study patients were responders (at least a 50% improvement in depressive symptoms) and 17% were remitters (minimal to no depressive symptoms). The results from a second rating scale of depression symptoms showed that 22% of the group were responders and 15% were remitters, and the results from a third rating scale showed that 32% were responders and 23% were remitters (see Table 2). It should be noted that about one in four or five people who were implanted with the device during the study were not included in these calculations of success at 12

Patient/Depression-30

months. Therefore it is possible that the percentage of patients having successful outcomes may be lower than is represented by the results described above.

7.1.3. Two-year results

After 2 years of VNS Therapy, the results showed that 32% of the patients were responders and 17% were remitters. The results from a second rating scale of depression symptoms showed that 27% of the group were responders and 13% were remitters (see Table 2). It should be noted that about one in three people who were implanted with the device during the study were not included in these calculations of success at 24 months. Therefore it is possible that the percentage of patients having successful outcomes may be lower than is represented by the results described above.

Table 2. Percent of Responders and Remitters After VNS Therapy

Standard-ized Test	HRSD$_{24}$		IDS-SR		MADRS	
	Responders	Remitters	Responders	Remitters	Responders	Remitters
3 months	15%	7%	14%	6%	17%	10%
12 months	30%	17%	22%	15%	32%	23%
24 months	32%	17%	27%	13%	N/A	N/A

Responders - ≥50% improvement in depressive symptoms.
Remitters – minimal to no depressive symptoms.

7.1.4. Additional categorization of clinical benefit

After 12 months of VNS Therapy, the patients were also assessed to categorize the degree of improvement in their depression symptoms. The amount of improvement was categorized as follows:

Worsened – depressive symptoms worse than when VNS Therapy was started

Minimal to no change – 0% to 24% improvement in depressive symptoms

Meaningful clinical benefit – 25% to 49% improvement in depressive symptoms

Highly meaningful clinical benefit – 50% to 74% improvement in depressive symptoms

Extraordinary clinical benefit – over 75% improvement in depressive symptoms

Figure 3 shows the percentage of patients who were in the different categories after 12 months of VNS Therapy. It should be noted that about one in four people who were implanted with the device during the study were not included in these calculations of success at 12 months. Therefore it is possible that the percentage of patients having successful outcomes may be lower than is represented by the results shown in the figure.

Patient/Depression-32

Figure 3. Categories of Clinical Benefit After 12 Months of VNS Therapy (HRSD$_{24}$)

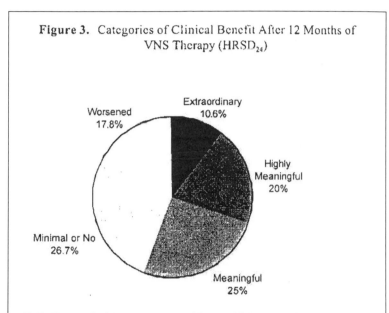

7.1.5.   Maintenance of benefit over time

Although less than one in three or one in four patients (depending on the rating scale used) appeared to respond to VNS Therapy, most—but not all—of those patients continued to be responders over time. For example, among the 30 patients who were responders on the HRSD$_{24}$ rating after their first 3 months of VNS Therapy, 60% continued to be responders after one year of VNS Therapy, and 70% were responders after two years of VNS Therapy. Among the 54 patients who were responders after 12 months of VNS Therapy, 69% continued to be responders after two years of VNS Therapy.

7.2. Quality of Life Measurements in the D-02 Clinical Study

In addition to improvements in depressive symptoms, patients who received VNS Therapy for one year in the D-02 study reported improvements in quality of life.

7.3. Expected Rate of Response to VNS Therapy

For patients in whom VNS Therapy is effective, the benefits are not always seen right away. In fact, the 12-week acute studies did not show a significant difference between patients receiving VNS Therapy and those who were not receiving it. Depressive symptoms may improve slowly over the first year of treatment.

7.4. Treatment Continuation Rates

Not all patients continue on VNS Therapy. During the D-02 study, 92% of the patients continued to receive therapy at 12 months and 82% continued to receive therapy at 24 months.

7.5. Limitations of VNS Therapy

VNS Therapy has not been shown to cure depression. It does not work for everyone. For most patients in whom it is effective, improvement in depressive symptoms will be slow (see "Expected Rate of Response to VNS Therapy" above). Some patients may have no change in symptoms with VNS Therapy, and some may actually get worse while receiving VNS Therapy. At present, doctors have no way to predict which patients will respond to VNS Therapy.

Patient/Depression-34

O

chapter nineteen

COMPARING ECT AND VNS

Although vagus nerve stimulation may sound sim-
ilar to electroconvulsive treatments (ECT), the two therapies are
entirely different. ECT is the most effective short-term therapy
currently available for severe depression. However, because of
fewer side effects and the substantially longer sustained response,
VNS Therapy™ will become the mainstream treatment for long-
term treatment of chronic depression.

History of electroconvulsive therapy

There is a stigma associated with electroconvulsive therapy
because early treatments used large electrical currents that caused
strong muscular contractions, which sometimes caused injury
(broken bones or dislocated joints). Moreover, the patients were
awake during the procedure—a terrifying experience. Everyone
remembers the dramatic (but no longer accurate) scenes in *One
Flew Over the Cuckoo's Nest*. Over the years the process has been
modified to maximize the benefit and minimize the side effects.
The amount of electricity has been decreased, patients are asleep

during the process, and muscle relaxants prevent muscle convulsions.

When is electroconvulsive therapy used?

Doctors prescribe ECT mainly to treat depression that does not respond to antidepressant medications and/or psychotherapy. While ECT is used in some cases to treat mania, schizophrenia, and catatonia, it is most useful in the treatment of depression. ECT can be the first choice of treatment for patients with psychotic depression (depression accompanied by hallucinations or delusions) and suicidal patients since it seems to start relieving symptoms after the first treatment, thereby reducing the risk of suicide.[1]

While the causes of depression are not known, abnormal chemical levels in the brain are believed to be involved. Electroconvulsive therapy is a shock treatment that induces a grand mal seizure in the brain. These seizures are similar to epileptic convulsions, where basically the brain's electrical pathways all fire at the same time. The seizure alters many chemical aspects of the brain during and after the seizure activity.

For ECT to be effective a series of treatments are required and a seizure must occur with each treatment. The patient typically receives electroconvulsive therapy three times a week for two to four weeks (at which time the depression should be gone). After several treatments, changes build up in the brain that relieve the depression. However, the changes in the brain are generally not permanent; CT scans and MRI scans taken before and after ECT show no structural changes in patient's brains. [2]

What happens during ECT?

Before an ECT treatment, patients receive a drug to put them to sleep and a muscle relaxant to prevent them from thrashing (and possibly hurting themselves) during the treatment. Patients feel nothing during ECT treatments since they are asleep.

Electrodes are placed on the head to deliver the electricity to the brain. Other electrodes on the body monitor the heart. The brain can be stimulated on one or both sides of the head, and the stimulation lasts for four seconds or less. The electricity induces the brain seizure, which lasts from 30 to 120 seconds. After the seizure ends, patients are allowed to wake up in a recovery room, and later go home until the next treatment.

What are the side effects of electroconvulsive therapy?

Side effects during electroconvulsive therapy include increased blood pressure and pulse, as well as irregular heartbeat. As with any procedure that requires anesthesia, there is a small risk of death (about 1 in 100,000). If the patient aspirates (breathes in) saliva or vomit they could develop pneumonia. In about 1 in 2,000 treatments the patient has spontaneous seizures after the end of the treatment.

When the patient wakes up after ECT, they may feel groggy, confused, nauseous, and have a headache and muscle aches. ECT also results in short-term memory loss and an impaired ability to retain new information (for example, they can't remember a new phone number). For most patients the problems with their memory usually ends a few weeks after the treatments end. However, in some cases long-term memory loss can occur.

How effective is electroconvulsive therapy?

ECT effectively ends episodes of depression in about 80 percent of patients who finish a course of ECT. However, since the brain changes that occur with electroconvulsive therapy are not permanent, there is a strong chance of the depression returning. In fact, with no further treatment, 90 percent of patients relapse in one year. Therefore, patients need further treatments, whether it is antidepressants, psychotherapy, or maintenance ECT (weekly or monthly ECT treatments).[3]

Is ECT the only choice for patients who do not respond to medication?

While ECT has been the last line of treatment for depressed patients who did not respond to antidepressant medications or psychotherapy, it does not work for all patients. In 1997, the FDA approved the vagus nerve stimulator for the treatment of epileptic seizures, and it has proved safe and effective for more than 30,000 patients. Research indicates it can also relieve treatment-resistant depression. In my opinion, vagus nerve stimulation will replace ECT as the treatment of choice. It should be noted that the treatments are complementary, so it is possible to have the VNS Therapy™ implant and "maintenance" ECT if needed.

Both ECT and the vagus nerve simulator use electrical stimulation of the brain to effect changes, but the mechanisms they use are very different. In electroconvulsive therapy, electrical stimulation of the brain causes a massive discharge of the nervous pathways in the brain, resulting in a grand mal seizure (similar to an epileptic seizure), temporarily altering the chemical makeup of the brain. The VNS Therapy Systems'™ pulse generator stimulates the vagus nerve, which in turn stimulates specific cells in the brain that favorably affect mood and depression. The pacemaker-like generator is preset to deliver stimulation to the vagus nerve on a continuous intermittent basis.

Although scientists do not know exactly how vagus nerve stimulation works, they do know that the continuous delivery of stimulation to the vagus nerve causes changes in key areas of the brain that affect depression.

One of the major problems with ECT is memory loss. The major side effect of vagus nerve stimulation is hoarseness, which is mild and tends to disappear over time. ECT therapy requires multiple treatments in a hospital setting; Vagus nerve stimulation requires one hospital visit to implant the stimulator. While ECT has been used for decades to treat depression, it is a cumbersome technique that has a strong negative stigma attached to it. The significant side effects and high relapse rate associated with ECT make it less than ideal.

Notes

1. *Electroconvulsive therapy: Treatment for depression.* Mayo Foundation for Medical Education and Research (MFMER)

2. Barklage, N. and Jefferson, J.W. *Electroconvulsive Therapy - A Guide.* 2002. Madison Institute of Medicine, Inc., Madison, WI 53717

3. *Electroconvulsive therapy: Treatment for depression.* Mayo Foundation for Medical Education and Research (MFMER)

AFTERWORD

Many authors who write memoirs about a disease they have or a challenge they've overcome conclude their stories by saying they are glad to have suffered and grateful for what they learned from the experience. I am not in any way grateful for my experience. Chronic depression is gruesome beyond words. It is pure hell. Instead, I will end this book the way I began it, with the *Larry King Show*.

As I write this epilogue, former President Bill Clinton (fellow Georgetown University alumnus and commencement speaker at my graduation in May 1980) is being interviewed by Mr. King about his 956-page memoir, *My Life*. Incredibly almost fifteen minutes of the program is devoted to the subject of depression.

I am amazed. A man who was president of the most powerful country in the world for eight years has tremendous insight into the horrifying disease of depression. He simply said some people can be helped with their depression and some can't—and there's nothing to explain the disparity. Outside the mental health community, there are few people who say and actually believe this to be true.

President Clinton's grasp of this baffling disease is remarkable. He talked about a former roommate of his who committed suicide; and the suicide of the Chief of Naval Operations during his administration, Admiral Mike Boorda. Boorda was found at home with a gunshot wound to the chest, a gun found nearby. Clinton praised the admiral as being the sailor's sailor and that he was the first enlisted man in the history of the country to rise to become chief of naval operations.

Of course he talked about the suicide of Vince Foster, deputy White House counsel during the Clinton administration. Clearly pained, the former president explained how he and Vince had been friends in Arkansas, since the ages of four and six. Vince suffered from depression, was under tremendous pressure, and he was being crucified in the press about Travelgate and Whitewatergate. He knew Vince was upset by a particular article published in the *Wall Street Journal* Op-Ed page about him; so he called Vince that night and invited him over to watch a movie, just as they had done many times as kids. Vince declined and said he just wanted to spend some time with his wife, Lisa. President Clinton said that, in retrospect, he was convinced Vince had already decided to commit suicide. The next day Vince shot himself through the back of his head.

After watching the show, I became extremely concerned about a close friend who suffers from terrible depression, including suicidal thoughts. She hadn't returned any of my phone calls in over a week. I drove over to her house the next day to make sure everything was okay. I walked in the door and, while I was extremely relieved to see her, I was visibly shaken. There I was, staring directly into the black hole—and it was scary. "I am doing just fine," she mumbled. I stayed for a few minutes and then drove back home, my heart pounding. I was terrified for her safety.

I called her as soon as I walked into my condominium. I pleaded with her to call me if she seriously contemplated acting upon her suicidal thoughts. I felt totally helpless. She didn't say anything. She could have said, "Yeah, I'll be sure to give you a ring right before I blow my brains out." But she spared me the embarrassment. I felt stupid, but what else could I have done?

Having been sufficiently humbled and reminded that I do not have qualifications in psychotherapy, I have set a much more modest goal for myself. I don't want to ever have to write the sequel to this book: *Return to The Black Hole.*

WRITTEN ON JULY 4, 2004

O
Epilogue

POST-FDA APPROVAL

I started writing this while watching QVC's "Count- down to Christmas" (91 days!) on television. The hosts were dressed in Christmas sweaters, wishing each other Merry Christmas, and trumpeting that over 49,000 of the Christmas "Deal of the Day" had sold during the past hour. After one of the hosts cheerily advised viewers that it is "never too early to start shopping for the holiday season," I decided to change the channel to a rerun of the 1970's television series *One Day at a Time*.

I have gone through many things since the 1970s; but nothing has been more important to me than the sustained response I continue to enjoy from VNS™ Therapy. I use the word enjoy, because that is how I personally define the benefit that I have derived from this treatment.

The July 15, 2005, approval of vagus nerve stimulation as an adjunctive therapy for treatment-resistant depression by the U.S. Food and Drug Administration gives you the option of a unique and effective treatment. Unlike traditional antidepressants, stimulation to the left vagus nerve induces widespread positive effects in key areas of the brain responsible for depression.

For many years I desperately hoped for something "different" to bring me *Out of the Black Hole*. I had lost confidence that a drug could rescue me from the grips of this disease. Almost five years after I was implanted with the vagus nerve stimulator, you now have the same option.

VNS has not made me bulletproof from the sad or stressful events that happen in life. The sadness from the death of a very close friend of thirty-three years, the stress of writing this book, or the daily pressure of maintaining the VagusNerveStimulator.com Website could have potentially sent me back to the mental health gutter. (Although self-publishing this book has made me a little nutty at times!)

The U.S. Food and Drug Administration's approval of VNS Therapy™ for chronic depression will change the lives of many TRD sufferers (and the lives of their families). Neurostimulation offers new hope to sufferers of many chronic diseases, including depression. Researchers and scientists have learned so much about the human brain since I was implanted with the VNS Therapy System™ in 2001. The research will continue long after the July 15, 2005, FDA approval.

I am confident that my remission will continue as well, ever cautious that the beast (depression) could rear its ugly head at any time. I am maintaining the strategy to improve myself both physically and mentally, but also spiritually. Fortunately, there is no need for me to write the sequel to this book: *Return to Black Hole*. TRD sufferers now have the option of VNS Therapy™ available to them. Many lives will be changed.

There is no book long enough to adequately express my gratitude for this therapy and for every one of my caretakers, who were by my side when I was so very ill.

To those who are reading this book in search of a solution to this debilitating disease, there is no right thing for me to say. We know there are many wrong things to say because we've heard them all. My hope is that my written words help make you feel less alone by relating to parts of my story and encouraging you to seek treatment.

Warm wishes.

WRITTEN ON SEPTEMBER 25, 2005

O

appendix a

NEUROLOGICAL DEVICES PANEL MEETING

UNITED STATES OF AMERICA
FOOD AND DRUG ADMINISTRATION
+ + + + +
NEUROLOGICAL DEVICES PANEL of the
MEDICAL DEVICES ADVISORY COMMITTEE
+ + + + +
Seventeenth Meeting
TUESDAY, JUNE 15, 2004
The Panel met at 8:00 a.m. at the Holiday Inn Gaithersburg,
Walker/Whetstone Rooms, Two Montgomery Village Avenue,
Gaithersburg, Maryland, Dr. Kyra J. Becker, Chairperson, presid-
ing.

PANEL MEMBERS PRESENT:
KYRA J. BECKER, M.D., Chairperson, University of
    Washington School of Medicine, Seattle, WA
ANDREW K. BALO, Industry Representative, DexCom, Inc.
    San Diego, California

JONAS H. ELLENBERG, Ph.D., Voting Member, Westat,
Rockville, Maryland

LAURA J. FOCHTMANN, M.D. Deputized Voting Member,
State University of New York, Stony Brook, NY

ANNAPURNI JAYAM-TROUTH, M.D., Voting Member,
Howard University College of Medicine, Washington, DC

RICHARD P. MALONE, M.D., Deputized Voting Member,
MCP Hanneman University, Philadelphia, PA

IRENE E. ORTIZ, M.D., Deputized Voting Member,
University of New Mexico, Albuquerque, NM

MARY LEE JENSEN, M.D., Director of Interventional
Neuroradiology, University of Virginia

PHILIP S. WANG, M.D., MPH, Dr.PH, Deputized Voting
Member, Brigham and Women's Hospital, Boston,MA

CRISSY E. WELLS, R.T., MBA, MHSA, Consumer
Representative, University of Virginia Health Sciences
Center, Charlottesville, VA

ALSO PRESENT:
CELIA WITTEN, Ph.D., M.D., Food and Drug
Administration, Division Director, General Restorative and
Neurological Devices

SPONSOR PRESENTERS:
RICHARD L. RUDOLPH, M.D., Vice President, Clinical
and Medical Affairs and Chief Medical Officer, Cyberonics
A. JOHN RUSH, M.D., Principal Investigator, University of
Dallas Southwestern MC, Dallas, TX
ALAN TOTAH, Vice President, Regulatory Affairs,
Cyberonics

FDA PRESENTERS:
CHANG LAO, Ph.D., Statistical Reviewer
CARLOS PENA, Ph.D., Neuroscientist, VNS Studies, Efficacy
Reviewer
MICHAEL SCHLOSSER, M.D., Neurosurgeon, Safety
Reviewer

PUBLIC SPEAKERS:
MARNA DAVENTORT, patient in the study
CHARLES DONOVAN, patient in the study
COLLEEN KELLY, patient in the study
LYDIA LEWIS, President, Depression and Bipolar Support
   Alliance
KARMEN McGUFFEE, patient in the study
IRVIN J. MUSZYNSKI, J.D., Director of the Office of Health
   Care Systems & Financing, American Psychiatric Association
LAURI SANDOVAL, patient in the study

INDEX

Brief Summary From the
Neurological Devices Panel Meeting

June 15, 2004

The Neurological Devices Panel (the Panel) met on Tuesday, June 15, 2004 in Gaithersburg, MD to discuss and make a recommendation to the Food and Drug Administration (FDA) on the approvability of the Cyberonics, Inc. PMA, P970003/S50 for the Vagus Nerve Stimulator (VNS) Therapy System intended for the adjunctive long-term treatment of chronic or recurrent depression for patients over the age of 18 who are experiencing a major depressive episode that has not had an adequate response to two or more antidepressant treatments. The Panel membership for this meeting consisted of four psychiatrists, one interventional neuroradiologist, two neurologists, a statistician, a consumer representative, and an industry representative.

The sponsor presented its information on the safety and effectiveness of the device, and FDA reviewers summarized the data in the PMA. After deliberations on the information in the submission, the Panel considered FDA's questions.

The Panel then voted five to two to recommend that FDA approve the PMA with conditions. The recommended conditions of approval are as follows:

1.   Patients should have failed four or more trials of traditional treatment modalities for treatment-resistant depression (medications and electroconvulsive therapy) prior to use of the device.

2.   The device be implanted by surgeons with appropriate training.

3.   Training regarding device electronic programming be provided for primary care providers.

4.   Additional patient labeling for use of the device and identification card be provided.

5.   A patient registry to collect clinical data be established.

6.   The physician labeling be revised regarding the following: 12 month open label follow-up, the variable effect of treatment, patient selection, and deletion of imaging claims.

The Panel members who voted against conditional approval believed a new study was necessary to establish a reasonable assurance of safety and effectiveness of the device.

Contact: Janet L. Scudiero, Executive Secretary, at 301-594-1184 ext. 176 or jls@cdrh.fda.gov.

Transcripts of this meeting may be purchased from:
Neal R. Gross and Company
1323 Rhode Island Ave., N.W.
Washington, D.C. 20005
202-234-4433 or 800-473-1433 and

Food and Drug Administration
Freedom of Information Staff (HFI-35)
5600 Fishers Lane, Rockville, MD 20857 301-443-1726 (fax)

Charles E. Donovan, III

May 10, 2004

Janet L. Scudicro
Center for Devices and Radiological Health (HFZ-410)
Food and Drug Administration
9200 Corporate Blvd.
Rockville, MD 20850

Re: Neurological Medical Devices Panel-June 15th, 2004

Dear Doctors,
I am a patient in the D-02 study and I am writing to urge you to do everything possible in your power to unconditionally approve the vagus nerve stimulator as a treatment for chronic depression. It not just saved my life (which I didn't really care about), it changed my life.

In the spring of 1980, I graduated from Georgetown University, ironically less than 30 minutes from where the Panel Meeting will take place. I also had my first major depressive episode that same spring. I had accepted a job in the Management Training Program of what is now JP Morgan Chase and moved to New York City after graduation.

I "bounced back" during that summer. But the depression was always there lurking in the background, and depressive episodes over time became more frequent.

To keep this letter short, let's fast forward 15 years. In November of 1995, I eventually ended up in the lock-up unit of a hospital. I have very little memory of the details surrounding this hospitalization. I can only assume that my family must have had the hell scared out of them and didn't know what to do.

In 1998, I was a 39 year-old man sobbing uncontrollably, hugging my parents in the doctor's office after the psychiatrist recommended shock treatments. I had a series of 15 or so. The ECT treatments did not work, nor did any of the countless antidepressants that I tried.

In late 1999, I was no longer able to work. I don't know how I was able to continue to work as long as I did. I put up a long hard fight. It was a big mistake. The physical toll and mental toll that it took on my body was agonizing and I am still recovering physically.

In 2001, I was implanted with the vagus nerve stimulator. In my final depression rating interview (just prior to implant) with Raymond Tait, Ph.D. of St. Louis University, I simply told him that I hoped that I would die on the operating table. Given the simplicity of the procedure, it was an irrational thing to hope for, but dying would have been the "ultimate escape".

I have no idea when the device was activated or how and when it was ramped up. As recently as just a few months ago, the study investigators told me that I may never know.

All I can say is that now my life is full of genuine happiness and joy. I don't have to fake it anymore. I have lost 30 pounds in the past 18 months. I exercise regularly; swimming, Pilates and running. I am not ashamed to go to a shopping mall or other public place for fear of being noticed. Last Saturday night I attended a small dinner party, that 18 months ago, I never would have gone to. I also am working on several different projects. This is the most productive that I have been in many years.

The improvement in mood occurred very gradually over many months. But, every morning I wake up and still ask myself the same question "Is it (the depression) back?" By the time I get in the shower, the answer is the same "NO". Because the mood improvement was gradual, there was no dramatic epiphany. At this point I would have to say that the most remarkable thing is the "staying power" of the therapy. It's like the Energizer Battery, it keeps going and going.

With the information learned from the studies and the benefit of stimulation "strategy" that new patients would have (that I did not have), many desperate patients could be helped.

Unless you have personally suffered from chronic depression, you cannot truly understand it. But it's brutal.

Again, I encourage you to approve this relatively straight forward procedure, for an extremely gruesome disease. Please give the option of vagus nerve stimulation therapy to those suffering patients who are still searching for an answer, just as I had searched. Some desperate patients stop searching-forever.

Respectfully,

Charles E. Donovan, III

O
appendix b

INSURANCE ISSUES

"One of the benefits of participating in the inves-tigational clinical trial for VNS Therapy was that I couldn't beat the price of the implant procedure: it was FREE. There was no fighting with an insurance company for pre-approvals; no in-network, out-of-network, or reimbursement issues; or having a bill kicked back unpaid after the treatment.

You, unfortunately, will not have that advantage. The good news, though, is I believe ultimately the majority of insurance companies will cover a large percentage, if not 100 percent, of the cost of VNS Therapy. Depending on where you live and other factors, the cost of the implant procedure, follow-up, changing the device settings, stimulation levels, etc., is around $25,000.

According to Cyberonics, 99.9 percent of all insurance companies cover the identical procedure for pharmaco-resistant epilepsy patients. Effective January 1, 2004, Medicare actually raised the level it reimburses hospitals for the VNS Therapy System™ by 23.7 percent, to just over $24,000. Effective January 1, 2005, Medicare again raised the reimbursement level—to

$24,645. This information is posted on the CMS (Centers for Medicare and Medicaid Services) Website: http://www.cms.hhs.gov and published in the Federal Register. In an environment where Medicare was slashing reimbursement rates across the board, this increase was a clear endorsement of the value of the VNS Therapy System™.

Because of Cyberonics' experience in epilepsy and negotiating reimbursement issues with insurance companies, a lot of the groundwork has been done for reimbursement for the depression indication. All of the major insurance companies are now familiar with the procedure. The only change is the diagnosis (chronic depression). I have listed below the insurance codes for the vagus nerve stimulator implant:

- The Stimulator: A4649
- The two incisions: 61885, 64573
- Intra-operative programming of VNS Therapy System: 95970, 05974, 95975

As we all know, insurance companies blatantly discriminate against mental health patients. I have tried to do my part by writing Congress to urge my support for passage of the Wellstone Mental Health Parity Act (see Appendix G). Unfortunately, Congress once again failed to reach an agreement on the passage of this critical piece of legislation in 2004. (Your Case Manager at Cyberonics will be invaluable to you in obtaining third-party reimbursement.)

An important part in approval decisions by third-party payers is the publication in prestigious peer-reviewed journals that the procedure is effective. The September 1, 2005, issue of *Biological Psychiatry* includes three articles about the data from the pivotal study of vagus nerve stimulation in treatment-resistant depression. The data was the foundation for issuance of final approval by the U.S. Food and Drug Administration (FDA) of vagus nerve stimulation as an adjunctive treatment for chronic depression. These articles, published in the official journal of the *Society for Biological Psychiatry*, confirm the association of VNS Therapy with significant antidepressant benefits that are sustained and/or growing over one year for patients with chronic or recurrent treatment-resistant depression.

Your Case Manager at Cyberonics can provide you the entire publication as part of the documentation package that you may need to submit to your insurance company in order to obtain approval for reimbursement.

Also, it is important that you check with the office of the insurance commissioner for your state. Some states require an appeal be submitted within thirty days of the denial.

It is impossible to predict exactly how insurance companies will reimburse VNS for depression. Insurance companies are giant bureaucracies, with multiple layers of people whose only job is to say no. Each insurance company is different; each policy is different. This potential challenge calls for reinforcements and you may need all the ammunition you can get. So, I have enlisted the help of the Patient Advocate Foundation. The Patient Advocate Foundation is a national non-profit organization that seeks "equal access to health care for all Americans." They are a superb, caring organization that truly puts the patient first.

Until reimbursement by third-party payers reaches the overall policy level, reimbursements decisions for VNS Therapy™ and depression will be made on a case-by-case basis. The Cyberonics Case Manager can interact with your insurance company or Medicare on your behalf. In addition, you will have to play an active role in getting your treatment approved and the Patient Advocate Foundation has provided a step-by step plan of action. On the following pages, I have reprinted a portion of the Foundation's *Your Guide to the Appeal Process*.

Your Guide To The Appeal Process
VOLUME II

Patient Advocate Foundation
700 Thimble Shoals Boulevard
Suite 200
Newport News, VA 23606
Tel: 757. 873.6668 1. 800.532.5274 Fax: 757.873.8999
Email: info@patientadvocate.org
Internet: http://www.patientadvocate.org/

MISSION STATEMENT
Patient Advocate Foundation is a national non-profit organization that
serves as an active liaison between the patient and their insurer, employer
and/or creditors to resolve insurance, job discrimination, and/or debt crisis
matters relative to their diagnosis through case managers and attorneys.
Patient Advocate Foundation seeks to safeguard patients through effective
mediation assuring access to care, maintenance of employment and preser-
vation of their financial stability.

ACKNOWLEDGMENTS
Your Guide to the Appeal Process was inspired by patients and family
members who work diligently at fighting a disease and for the right to
treatment. The Patient Advocate Foundation would like to thank the doctors, nurses, and other professionals who assist patients and their families
in these battles everyday. We would especially like to thank patients and
professionals who were willing to discuss their needs and concerns which
brought about the idea for this brochure.

Patient Advocate Foundation would like to gratefully acknowledge the
generous support of Amgen, Inc. in underwriting the research of the first
edition of *Your Guide to the Appeal Process* through an unrestricted educa-
tional grant.

We thank Janet Patton, RN, BSN, a Patient Advocate Foundation
employee, for her writing of this book. We express our gratitude to the
following members of our Editorial Review Board:

John D. Blum, Associate Dean for Health Law Programs Loyola University,
Chicago Illinois Professor of Law

Marc DeBofsky, Esq., DeBofsky & DeBofsky, Chicago, Illinois

Howard B. Hellen, Esq. San Diego, California

Marc Lippman, MD, Georgetown University Medical Center, Washington, DC

Richard P. Neuworth, Esq., Lebau & Neuworth, LLC, Baltimore, Maryland

The Patient Advocate Foundation would like to thank the Editorial Review Board for their thoughtful review, insightful comments, and expert advice.

Your Guide To The Appeal Process

INTRODUCTION

Dealing with an injury or illness is stressful for the patient as well as the family. When you or a loved one are denied a medical procedure or therapy that has been performed or requested to be performed by your treating physician, it can precipitate a crisis situation. Since each insurance policy is different, it would be impossible to write a fail proof plan that would work for each patient in all situations. Each patient and each situation is unique. This brochure is designed to help patients and their loved ones navigate the appeal process. It contains suggestions and advice. It should not be interpreted as a substitute for legal counsel.

It is also important to point out that support from your treating physician and specialist is critical. Your physician is the professional trained to assess and recommend a treatment plan for you.

Simply stated, a "denial" means that the insurance company has decided not to pay for the procedure or therapy that your doctor has recommended. The procedure or therapy may have already been performed or may be scheduled in the near future. If the denied procedure has not yet been performed, the insurer may be denying the request for pre-authorization. "Pre-authorization" means that the insurer has given approval for a member to receive a treatment, test, or surgical procedure before it has actually occurred. The goal of the appeal process is to allow the patient to be heard and provide any and all necessary information to convince the insurance company to change their decision and provide coverage for the procedure. This brochure is also designed to provide a logical approach to the appeal process. When submitting your appeal, keep in mind that the best defense is a good offense. In other words, it is generally better to take the time to gather all the necessary information and submit a well thought out appeal packet than to hastily submit a response and miss the opportunity to educate the insurance company about your specific situation. There are several steps you should take to produce a thorough appeal packet. These steps are:

1. gather preliminary information
2. understand the illness and the insurance
3. write the appeal letters
4. evaluate the result

Step 1: Gather Preliminary Information

If you do not already have a file and a notebook to document all correspondence, start one now. You should keep a record of all letters you receive and a log of all telephone calls you make or receive related to the denial. Over time you may forget people's names and dates. This documentation will help you stay organized and focused on your goal. There are specific questions you need to ask once you are notified the procedure will not be covered through pre-authorization.

- When did you receive notice of the denial?
- How did you receive notification of the denial?
- Did your doctor notify you directly, or did the administrator or insurer notify you directly?
- Did you receive a letter or phone call from the insurance company?
- Did you receive a statement from your insurance company stating that your bills will not be paid?

First and foremost, **you need to get a copy of the denial letter.** Under the Employee Retirement and Income Security Act (ERISA), your denial letter should include a **specific reason** for the denial and a reference to your plan explaining the basis for the denial. For example, is your insurance company denying paying for your treatment because it considers it to be experimental? Or, do you belong to an HMO that does not have out-of-network benefits and you wish to go to an out-of-network provider? Place a call to the doctor's office and find out what information was submitted to the insurance company and ask for a copy of the information and the letter written by your doctor requesting payment authorization. If your requests are ignored, you should put them in writing to make a record of your attempts to obtain the information you need.

If you have received a denial for a procedure that has already taken place and there are bills that are unpaid, you need to begin to backtrack to find out why.

- Does your insurance company require procedures to be pre-authorized?
- If so, did your doctor's office pre-authorize the procedure?

This brings up the most important documents you have and need: your plan document and plan summary, or health insurance booklets. The plan document and plan summary are essentially a contract between you and the insurance company. You need to be sure that you have a current copy. If you do not have a copy, you must write to the plan administrator and request that a copy be sent to you. Under ERISA, these documents must be sent to you within thirty days of the written request or the company may be assessed penalties. **READ** your plan language. What does it say about your procedure and specific reason for denial? Under ERISA, a specific reason for denial must be stated in language that would be understandable to an employee. If the procedure was to be pre-authorized, do you or does your doctor have a copy of the authorization or the approval from the insurance company? If no pre-authorization was required review specific exclusions listed in your plan. If your treatment is not identified as a specific exclusion, you need to begin your appeal.

- Who can you contact to discuss the denial?

Step 2: Understand the Illness and The Insurance

You need specific names and numbers of contact people. The denial letter from the insurance company may contain this information. You may need to call the insurance company and ask for a contact person. Be sure to ask for that person's direct line. Ask the staff at your doctor's office who you can call to ask questions and get any letters or records you may need. If you will be receiving your treatment at a facility away from home, be sure to have the name and number of your treating doctor's nurse. You will likely need to get letters from the treating doctor as well. You also need to be sure that you have a written copy of the steps that you must take in order to appeal the denial. This information should be in your plan document. It may also be in the denial letter. You may need to request this information from the insurance company. Be sure you understand each step of the appeal process. It is your path to obtaining reimbursement.

By answering these questions and collecting these documents you have the initial information you need. You have your plan document, your denial letter and you have the names of the contact people at the insurance company and the doctor's office. Now you must begin to educate yourself and continue to research the issue to achieve your goal of reimbursement. If you still do not understand your rights or the appeal process is unclear, and the employer or insurer will not or cannot explain further, it may be helpful to contact an attorney. (See "When to Consult an Attorney")

You need to understand your condition or your loved one's condition before you can discuss the case with the insurance company. It is very important that you understand exactly what the doctor wants to do and why it is necessary. Read any copies of the letters your doctor may have submitted to the insurance company. The initial letter typically discusses the patient's case in simple medical terms and then explains what the doctor proposes to do. This letter is often referred to as the "treatment plan" or "plan of care". You can also ask your doctor or nurse to explain it further. Often they may have written material that may be helpful, or they may be able to direct you in finding more information.

You need to be familiar with the type of insurance you have. If your insurance is through your employer or your spouse's employer, call the benefits manager and ask him or her to explain the coverage. For example, is the employer self-insured and does the employer contract with a third party to administer the plan? Or does the employer contract with an outside company to administer the plan **and** pay the claims? It makes a difference because you may be able to get your denial overturned by working with the benefits manager or the designated representative of Human Resources. If the company is not self-insured, explaining the problem to the benefits manager, both verbally and in writing, may be very beneficial. The benefits manager can, in some situations, put enough pressure on the insurance company to get the denial overturned. Also, if the employer has had problems with the insurer they may choose not to renew the contract with that insurance company.

Step 3: Write the Appeal Letters

After you have gathered the preliminary information and have a basic understanding of the illness and the insurance policy, you are ready to start the appeal process. Some appeals are handled by the doctor's office or the clinic or the hospital. In this situation, the patient is usually put in contact with a case manager who has experience in the appeals process. In this case, the patient should understand the steps in the process and should "oversee" what is being done. It is suggested that the patient request copies of all letters and correspondence to and from the insurer. The patient should also be in close contact with the case manager or person handling the appeal for them.

In other situations, the patient and family are informed of the denial and they must handle the appeal on their own. If this is the case, you must manage your appeal. Your appeal should include:

- An appeal letter.
- A letter from your doctor and specialist addressing specifics of your case.
- Any pertinent information from your medical records.
- Any articles from peer-reviewed clinical journals that support your case that illustrate medical efficacy.

Your Appeal Letter

The purpose of the appeal letter is to tell the insurance company that you disagree with their decision and why you believe they should cover the procedure. The letter should be factual and written in a firm but pleasant tone. When writing your appeal letter you should include:

- *Your identification.* This includes your policy number, group number, claim number, or other information used to identify your case.

- The reason for the denial that they explained in the denial letter.

- A brief history of the illness and necessary treatment. Typically this information will be included in the doctor's letter in detail but it can also be helpful to add a shorter and less complicated version in the patient's letter.

- The correct information. If you believe the decision was made because of an error, state the correct information, i.e. is the denied procedure different from the requested procedure? Maybe a coding error was made and the insurance company believes you will be receiving a different drug.

- Why you believe the decision was wrong. Specific information based on facts to show that the treatment should be provided, i.e. you may have to go out-of-network for a procedure but only because the procedure is medically necessary according to your doctor and there is no in-network provider for the treatment.

- What you are asking the insurance company to do. Typically you are asking that the insurer reconsider the denial and approve coverage for the procedure in a timely manner.

Sample Appeal Letters

The Sample Appeal Letters included in this guide are designed to be a general guide for your specific letter. Sample Appeal Letter A was written as though the denial was based on a question of medical necessity. Sample Appeal Letter B addresses the issue of a denial based on "out of network" benefits. Each patient and each denial are unique. It is recommended that you read each letter and then identify other important details that need to be added to your letter. You must also remain factual. It is very important that your denial letter be focused on the intended outcome.

Sample Letter A

[Date]

[Name]
[Insurance Company Name] [Address]
[City, State ZIP]
Re: [Patient's Name] [Type of Coverage]
[Group number / Policy Number]

Dear [Name of contact person at insurance company],

Please accept this letter as [patient's name] appeal to [insurance company name]'s decision to deny coverage for [state the name of the specific procedure denied]. It is my understanding based on your letter of denial dated [insert date] that this procedure has been denied because:

[Quote the specific reason for the denial stated in the denial letter.]

As you know, [patient's name] was diagnosed with [disease] on [date]. Currently Dr. [name] believes that [patient's name] will significantly benefit from [state procedure name]. Please see the enclosed letter from Dr. [name] that discusses [patient's name]'s medical history in more detail.

[Patient's name] believes that you did not have all the necessary information at the time of your initial review. [Patient's name] has also included with this letter, a letter from Dr. [name] from [name of treating facility]. Dr. [name] is a specialist in [name of specialty]. [His/Her] letter discusses the procedure in more detail. Also included are medical records, and several journal articles explaining the procedure and the results.

Based on this information, [patient's name] is asking that you reconsider your previous decision and allow coverage for the procedure Dr. [name] outlines in [his/her] letter. The treatment is scheduled to begin on [date]. Should you require additional information, please do not hesitate to contact [patient's name] at [phone number]. [Patient's name] will look forward to hearing from you in the near future.

Sincerely,

Sample Letter B

[Date]

[Name]
[Insurance Company Name] [Address]
[City, State ZIP]
Re: [Patient's Name] [Type of Coverage]
[Group number / Policy Number]

Dear [Name of contact person at insurance company],

Please accept this letter as my appeal to [insurance company name]'s decision to deny coverage for [state the name of the specific procedure denied]. It is my understanding based on your letter of denial dated [insert date] that this procedure has been denied because:

[Quote the specific reason for the denial stated in the denial letter.]

I have been a member of your [state name of PPO, HMO, etc.] since [date]. During that time I have participated within the network of physicians listed by the plan. However, my primary care physician, Dr. [name] believes that the best care for me at this time would be [state procedure name]. At this time there is not a physician within the network who has extensive knowledge of this procedure. Dr. [name of primary care physician], a plan provider, has recommended that I have the procedure done outside the network by Dr. [name of specialist] at [name of treatment facility].

I have enclosed a letter from Dr. [name of primary care physician] explaining why he recommends [name of procedure]. I have also enclosed a letter from Dr. [name of specialist] explaining the procedure in detail, his qualifications and experience, and several articles that discuss the procedure.

Based on this information, I am asking that you reconsider your previous decision and allow me to go out-of-network to Dr. [name] for [name of specific procedure]. The procedure is scheduled to begin on [date]. Should you require additional information, please do not hesitate to contact me at [phone number]. I look forward to hearing from you in the near future.

Sincerely,

Your Doctor's Appeal Letter

You should also ask your doctor and your specialist to write a letter discussing your specific case and why your treatment is medically necessary. The letter should be addressed to the person at the insurance company that sent you the denial letter, or directly to the medical director at the insurance company.

It should include:

- Any information about your illness that your doctor feels is clinically important.
- The prescribed treatment plan.
- Why the treatment is medically necessary.

Medical Records

Ask your doctor and specialist if there are any documents in your medical records that may be helpful in your appeal. For example, it may be helpful to send a pathology result documenting the specific cell type. In the case of certain cancers, the insurance company may need to see what chemotherapy drugs you have already received. In some cases the insurance company may ask to see specific documents from your medical records.

Articles from peer-reviewed clinical journals

Often an insurance company will deny a procedure because they believe there is not enough evidence that the procedure is helpful for a specific disease. If you and your doctor believe this is the basis for your denial, you need to submit documentation that the procedure is effective. This documentation should be in the form of articles that come from the professional journals or "magazines" that doctors use to keep up to date on the latest treatments. These journals have editorial boards of physicians who specialize in specific areas of medicine. That is what makes a journal "peer reviewed". This type of documentation has become very popular with the insurance companies and it is very common for them to request this type of documentation. Your physician and specialist have probably had such a request for information in the past and they can assist you in obtaining these articles.

These four pieces of information should be put together in a

Physician's Sample Appeal Letter

[Date]

[Name]
[Insurance Company Name] [Address]
[City, State ZIP]

Re: [Patient's Name] [Type of Coverage]

[Group number / Policy Number]

Dear [Name of contact person at insurance company],

It is my understanding that [Patient's name] has received a denial for [name of procedure] because it is believed that the procedure is [state specific reason for the denial i.e. not medically necessary, experimental, etc.].

As you know, [patient's name] has been under my care since [date] for the treatment of [state disease]. [Give a brief medical history emphasizing the most recent events that directly influence your decision to recommend the denied therapy.]

For this reason I am writing to provide you with information regarding [name of procedure]. [Give a brief, yet specific description of the procedure and why you believe it should be approved.]

I have also included several journal articles supporting the use of [name of procedure] for [patient's name] [name of disease].

I ask that you reconsider your previous decision based on the information above. I believe therapy should begin on [date]. Should you have any questions, please do not hesitate to call me at [phone number].

Sincerely,

"packet" and be submitted to the insurance company by registered mail or some other form that you will be able to track and find out who signed for the information. This will alleviate the excuse that the information was "never received". You should keep a duplicate copy of all the information you are submitting and add it to your file. You may wish to call to confirm receipt of your materials.

After the denial has been received and your appeal has been submitted, the next thing to do is wait for a response. Waiting can be the hardest part. Your plan probably gives a length of time that the insurance company has to respond to your appeal. If it does not, you need to ask the benefits manager or the insurance company when you will be notified of the response. If you are unable to get a response, you may want to consider legal counsel. (see "When to Consult an Attorney")

Sample Appeal Letters

The Physician 's Sample Appeal Letter is also a general guide for a specific letter. Most physicians have written appeal letters many times. Some are far removed from the appeal process and are unsure of the specifics of your denial. They may also be unsure of the amount of information necessary. It is important that you communicate the specific reason for the denial to your treating physician and ask that they write their appeal letter with enough information to address the denial specifically.

Step 4: Evaluate The Result

If you receive a phone call or a letter informing you that your denial has been overturned and the insurance company will cover the procedure, CONGRATULATIONS! Before you celebrate you need to request a copy of the approval letter. You also need to be sure that you are aware of any conditions that are included. For example, you may get an approval to have the surgical procedure, but the insurance company may only cover it if it is performed by one of the doctors in their plan that you have never seen. If the conditions are unreasonable and unacceptable to you, discuss them with your doctor and insurance contact person. You may consider continuing with the appeal process. Most plans have several levels of appeal.

If your appeal has been denied, you also need a copy of the second denial letter. Like your original denial letter, this letter must also contain the specific reason for denial. Read the letter carefully. It may have a different reason for the denial. For example, the original denial letter states that a bone marrow transplant was denied because it was not effective for the disease, and was to be performed "out-of network". You submitted your appeal and all the appropriate documentation. The second denial letter rejects the procedure because "there was not enough evidence provided to show that the transplant is medically necessary". These are very different reasons for denying the same procedure.

Typically, the second level of appeal will be reviewed by a different group of people at the insurance company. Usually your second denial letter will explain the reason for denial and may even ask that you submit specific information that was not received with your first appeal letter. Be sure to notify your doctor of the decision and the new information that is needed. This denial letter may instruct that if you are interested in appealing further that you send your letter and new information to a different person. If you decide to continue with the appeal process, you should submit another appeal packet with new information specifically addressing the current reason for denial. Again, keep copies of all information and send the packet registered mail, return receipt requested. If your appeal is again denied, you should request the third denial in writing and notify your doctor. If you believe your insurance company should cover the procedure and are willing to proceed with the appeal process, you should refer to your plan document for the next step.

At this point some insurance companies will offer you what they call an "external review". This means that the insurance company will send your appeal to a company that they contract with who will review the denial, the appeal, and any new information and make a recommendation to the insurance company about the procedure in question. The external review board is typically made up of nurses, attorneys, and doctors who specialize in the specific procedure you are asking the insurance company to cover. In some states the law allows the patient to request that your case be sent for an external review. To date, the following states have external review boards:

Arizona	California	Connecticut
Florida	Hawaii	Illinois
Maryland	Minnesota	Missouri
New Jersey	New Mexico	New York
Ohio	Pennsylvania	Rhode Island
Tennessee	Texas	Vermont

If you live in a state who has an external review board, you can contact the state department of insurance for further information.

While external review can be very beneficial, it is important that the limitations are clear. The external review company can only act within specific parameters. They cannot override your policy. They can make decisions based on your policy guidelines. For example, you need to have surgery and want an "out-of-network" doctor miles from your town to perform the surgery but you have a policy with no out-of-network benefits. Your insurance company agrees that you need the surgery and has an in-network surgeon in your town. If the surgeon in your town is in-network and is qualified to perform the surgery the external review board would probably not be helpful because of the nature of your request. However, if you and your surgeon believe that the surgeon in your town is not qualified to perform the surgery for a specific reason and you can support this with the necessary documentation, the external review board may be able to substantiate your claim. That may result in the insurance company overturning your denial.

At this point, if you have exhausted all the levels of appeal and are not satisfied with the decision, your remaining alternative may be to pursue the issue in court.

When to Consult an Attorney

This is an important question and one that is asked frequently. There is no right or wrong answer. Many people feel more secure discussing their case with an attorney when they receive the denial. Others would rather appeal the decision on their own to see if they can overturn it without legal help and expense. For some it depends on the cost of the procedure that has been denied. It may make more sense to seek legal advice if the procedure costs $100,000 than if the procedure costs $1000. As previously mentioned, if you do not understand the appeal process or you are unable to get answers from your employer or insurance company, an attorney may be helpful to advise you of your rights and options. This is an individual decision. If you decide to seek legal advice you should consider the following:

- Select an attorney with experience in healthcare law.
- Discuss the legal fees up front and request a detailed billing.
- Determine at what point the attorney will take over the case.

Some patients will completely exhaust the administrative appeal process before they ask an attorney to take over the case. It is imperative that you make every effort to have an attorney involved in the case throughout the administrative appeal process in the event you wish to pursue the case later in court.

Others to Notify

Insurance and patient's rights are a hotly debated political issue. Patients often ask if it is helpful to notify their state and local representatives of their insurance issues. In some cases it has been helpful. Other times, patients get nothing more in return than a form letter stating there is nothing their legislator can do. You may choose to approach this question by asking yourself, "What do I have to lose?" You are already preparing your own appeal letter. You could easily send a copy of your denial letter and your appeal letter to your legislators asking for any assistance they can provide. You may access a list of legislators by state at the PAF website: http://www.npaf.org.

It may also be beneficial to notify your State Department of Insurance. The duties of the insurance commissioner and the Department of Insurance vary from state to state. One of the main objectives is to be sure the insurance company is following the patient's policy. The Department of Insurance may also be aware of any state laws that may come in to play in a specific case. Many states require that problems be reported by the patient in writing and may even require that their forms be filled out. It can be helpful to notify the Department of Insurance in your state when you receive the original denial. You can call them to request a copy of the necessary paperwork to submit your complaint.

In some rare instances it may be necessary to contact the media. This is recommended only if you have tried at length to resolve the problem and have enlisted the help of your legislators and the Department of Insurance with no resolution.

Expedited Review

If you have received a denial for a procedure that must be performed within a specific time frame, you and your doctor need to communicate that to the insurance company immediately. Most states have laws protecting patients in an emergency. That may be different if the procedure must be started in near future. Most insurance companies already have a plan in place for such occurrences and their guidelines will be different. If you do not feel that you are making progress toward your goal and time is short, you may choose to consult an attorney to advise you of your rights and options.

When to Contact the Patient Advocate Foundation

You may contact the PAF at any point in the process for our advice, guidance, and support. The appeals process is very complicated. It requires you to gather information and write letters. You need to keep a notebook and a file for documentation. You need to remain courteous and polite when working with your insurance company, while you are dealing with the stress of an illness. You now know what steps to take to appeal your denial. Take this process one step at a time.

Take it one day at a time. The PAF would be happy to answer any questions you may have. To reach the Patient Advocate Foundation:

753 Thimble Shoals Blvd., Suite B
Newport News, Virginia 23606
Tel: 1.800.532.5274 -or- 757.873.6668
FAX: 757.873.8999
E-mail: help@patientadvocate.org
Internet: www.patientadvocate.org

References

Aetna will allow members to appeal denials. (1999) Associated Press. http: //www. insure. com/health/zzaetnareview 199.html

Decarlo, T. (April, 1999) The top ten HMO mistakes, how to avoid them. New Woman, pp. 86-119.

Frey, H. (1998). How to protect yourself in the age of managed care. http://www.patientadvocacy.net/pac4.htm

Greene, Jan. (1998) Some HMOs now let you appeal. http://www.onhealth.com/ch1/columnist/item,34478.asp

Help for health insurance customers. (1999) National Association of Insurance Commissioners.

http://www.insure.com/health/naic-kit998.html

Never talk to the monkey when the organ grinder is available. (January, 1998). http://www.integsoft.com/appeals/tal/monkey.htm

Practical Tips for the Practicing Oncologist. (1997) American Society of Clinical Oncology. Chapter 18, pp. 83-84.

Reimer, S. (1995). What to do when denied health or disability benefits. (Spring, 1995) The CFIDS Chronicle, p. 37.

Taking control of your health care. A guide to getting the most from your health plan. Pamphlet by: Citizens for the "Right to Know".

Timely solutions for improving oncology provider case manager communications. (1998). Independent Study module by Oncology Education Services.

You have a VOB, now make 'em pay. (January, 1998) http://www.integsoft.com/appeals/tal/vob.htm

O

appendix c

MEDICARE PART D

Reprinted with permission.

Patient Advocate Foundation
help@patientadvocate.org
700 Thimble Shoals Blvd
Suite 200
Newport News, VA 23606
Phone: (800) 532-5274
Fax: (757) 873-8999

What does Medicare Part D Mean for Me?

Starting January 1, 2006, the Centers for Medicare & Medicaid Services (CMS) will extend coverage for prescription drugs to Medicare beneficiaries.

Medicare Part D is the new prescription drug benefit resulting from the Medicare Modernization Act of 2003, providing all beneficiaries with the option to add prescription drug coverage. A premium will be charged for Part D in the same way there is a premium for Part B benefits.

You will have to pay a premium each month for the Part D benefit. The premium for Part D is approximately $35-37 a month. Each enrollee wishing to participate will have to elect Part D coverage and choose a corresponding Prescription Drug Plan (PDP) or a Medicare Advantage Plan (MA-PD). Those beneficiaries with limited income and resources may be able to get additional help for monthly premiums, deductibles and co-payments.

To learn more about Medicare Part D, please click here to view our brochure entitled Medicare Modernization Act of 2003's Prescription Drug Coverage through Part D

How Do I Get This Additional Help?

Additional financial assistance will be available for people with low incomes and limited assets. Medicare beneficiaries who have incomes below a certain limit will not have to pay premiums or deductibles for prescription drugs.

1. If you have both Medicare and Medicaid with prescription drug coverage, Medicare and Supplemental Security Income, or if your state pays for your Medicare premiums, you automatically will get this extra help. At this time you do not have to do anything.

2. If your annual income is below $14,355 for an individual ($19,245 for a married couple living together), you may not have to pay monthly premiums or deductibles, and you could pay as little as $2 for your co-payments. You will need to fill out an application for assistance.

3. For all others that do not meet the requirements above, you still can apply for assistance for your monthly premiums, annual deductibles and prescription co-payments. After you apply, Social Security will review your application and send you a letter to let you know if you qualify for assistance through Medicare Part D.

**Information above taken straight from "Help Available to Pay Costs of Medicare's New Prescription Drug Program" written by the Social Security Administration.

How Do I Apply?

Mail - Many Medicare beneficiaries who may be eligible for the additional help will be mailed an Application for Help with Medicare Prescription Drug Plan Costs (Form SSA-1020) from now until August 2005.

If you receive an application, please complete it and return it as soon as possible. If you do not receive an application, you can get one by calling Social Security at 1-800-772 1213 (TTY 1-800-325-0778).

Phone - Patient Advocate Foundation has clinical case managers able to answer your questions and assist in the application process of the Medicare Part D benefit. Please call PAF at 1-800 532-5274.

Online - If you would like to apply online, an online application will be available July 1st at www.socialsecurity.gov.

How Will I Know If I Qualified?

After you apply, Social Security will review your application and send you a letter to let you know if you qualify for the additional help. If you qualify, you need to enroll in a Medicare-approved prescription drug plan to get help with your prescription costs. You can select a plan between November 15, 2005, and May 15, 2006.

**Information above taken straight from "Help Available to Pay Costs of Medicare's New Prescription Drug Program" written by the Social Security Administration.

Have Questions?

If you have questions regarding Medicare benefits, Patient Advocate Foundation provides access to a clinical case manager who is available to answer your individual questions Monday through Friday. If you need assistance please click here to submit your questions and we will research your issue and provide a response in 24-48 hours. If you would like to speak with a case manager or if you would like to apply for Medicare Part D benefits, please call 1-800-532-5274 and a case manager will return your call.

# # #

Medicare Rx Plans Set To Go Public; Average Formulary Covers 88% Of Seniors' Top Drugs

October 03, 2005
Volume 01 | Number 003

Organizations offering Medicare prescription drug coverage will cover "the vast majority of all commonly used" products, Centers for Medicare & Medicaid Services Administrator Mark McClellan said Sept. 30 as he unveiled the details of Part D drug plan benefits.

McClellan spoke at a briefing one day before stand-alone prescription drug plans (PDPs) and Medicare Advantage Drug Plans (MA-PDs) could begin marketing to the public. CMS posted state-by-state lists on its website, giving the name of each PDP and MA-PD with its monthly premium, drug deductible (zero, reduced, or the standard $250), whether it includes tiered copayments for drugs, whether additional coverage is offered in the coverage gap, if mail-order pharmacy is offered, and how many of the top 100 drugs used by seniors are on the plan formulary.

CMS had withheld most plan details until Sept. 30 so that all plans would come out of the starting gate together for marketing. Enrollment begins Nov. 15.

McClellan and other CMS officials held additional briefings the same day with Medicare stakeholders to congratulate them on the program's development and to rally them for working with the public at this critical turning point for the program.

Regarding drug formularies, McClellan said that "on average, plans are covering about 88% of the top 100 drugs" for seniors. Overall, coverage is at least "generally in the upper 70s or higher and many plans cover essentially all of the available drugs." CMS will release more extensive information on formularies during the first week of October.

Also that week, CMS will begin mailing local editions of the *Medicare & You* handbook to beneficiaries. In addition to describing the drug benefit, the handbook will list the different plans beneficiaries can choose from if they decide to participate in the Part D drug benefit. Ten companies will market nationwide PDPs (see story in *Medicare Drug Focus*, Sept. 26, 2005).

McClellan urged beneficiaries to concentrate on comparing plans based on their own preferences about premiums, deductibles and other plan design features—and not to focus on the "standard" benefit required by the Medicare Modernization Act. He emphasized that competition among plan sponsors has yielded an abundance of plans available to most seniors, many or perhaps even most of which "go beyond" the standard minimum.

"Everyone in Medicare, no matter what their income or how they get their health care, can choose the coverage that reflects what they want," McClellan declared. "They can make their choices based on lower costs, on more complete coverage and on convenient access."

Every State Has A Reduced Deductible Plan

For example, potential enrollees in every state will be offered at least one plan with a deductible less than the $250 standard benefit, and often a plan with no deductible.

"In every state" as well, CMS reported, "Medicare beneficiaries will have options that include coverage in the standard benefit's 'coverage gap'" or so-called "donut hole," — the standard benefit's requirement that a senior pay the entire cost of drugs between the first $2,250 in total spending and the $5,100 catastrophic coverage threshold. MA-PDs in all states but nine also offer coverage in the gap; those nine are Connecticut, Idaho, Iowa, Maine, Nebraska, New Hampshire, North Carolina, North Dakota, and South Dakota.

"If you don't want a donut hole, you can choose a plan that fills that in," often by covering generic products and sometimes even covering more expensive, brand-name products, McClellan said. The choices counter early concerns that deductibles and the coverage gap could deter participation, the CMS chief suggested.

CMS continues to highlight the lower-than-expected premiums for drug coverage. "There are plans available for under $20 in every state [except Alaska]â€¦ including under $10 in many states," McClellan noted.

Northern Plain States, Where Some Predicted Benefit Would Fail, Have Affordable Options

McClellan singled out the northern plain states - region 25 (Iowa, Minnesota, Montana, Nebraska, North Dakota, South Dakota, and Wyoming)—where stand-alone PDP coverage is available for a $1.87 monthly premium. Early skeptics had questioned whether companies would seek to provide drug coverage at all in such states, he noted.

Humana is the organization offering the $1.87 premium. A look at the plan choices in North Dakota alone illustrates the myriad information seniors will sort through and weigh when selecting a plan.

The $1.87 premium is for a "standard" coverage stand-alone PDP. Humana also is offering an "enhanced" PDP with a $4.91 monthly premium and a "complete" PDP for a $38.70 premium.

The standard package includes the $250 deductible, while the other two have a zero deductible. The formulary for all three Humana options includes 97 of seniors' top 100 drugs, but only the complete package provides additional coverage in the gap. That additional coverage includes both brand-name and generic products. North Dakotans have 41 different PDPs to choose from, plus seven MA-PDs.

All beneficiaries have to pay a Part B outpatient services premium to participate in Medicare Advantage, but nearly three-quarters now can choose an MA-PD with no additional cost for the drug benefit and, in many cases, enhanced benefits for hospital and medical care. McClellan predicted that 2006 may turn out to be a "phenomenal year" for MA-PDs.

Some Contracts Still Await Signing At CMS

Medicare & You will list the MA-PDs and also their care model, such as health maintenance organization or preferred provider organization. Also, CMS will soon list which options are available in each county, since many PPOs are organized on a more local level.

Other factors beneficiaries might consider include copayments, coverage of the individual's favorite pharmacy, availability of mail-order pharmacy and coverage in different states for those who may have two residences. Many plans are offering a flat copayment or a tiered copayment. The latter usually sets three or four levels of copayments, with the lowest for generic drugs, then increasing for preferred brand drugs, nonpreferred brand drugs and, sometimes, for high-cost specialty products such as biotechnology-based drugs, McClellan explained.

"Now that we're delivering the benefits," McClellan said, "we are turning our focus to providing comprehensive support to help beneficiaries make a confident decision to take advantage of this drug coverage." In addition to *Medicare & You* and the 1-800-MEDICARE call center, the agency will aid beneficiaries in making choices through web-based tools such as the Plan Finder.

The tools should be available Oct. 14. CMS also expects the cable network CNBC to televise a "town hall" session on the drug benefit Nov. 19.

Nonetheless, at least a few plan contracts are still on the desk at CMS. In a teleconference with participating plans, CMS Senior Advisor to the Administrator Abby Block said some contracts still have details to be ironed out and the agency will establish a "regular update schedule" to ensure that new approvals are communicated.

~ Denise Peterson

O

appendix d

PSYCHOLOGY TODAY MAGAZINE'S 101 FACTS ABOUT DEPRESSION

The following information is reprinted with permission from *Psychology Today's Blues Buster: The Newsletter About Depression*, May 2004. Here is the latest information about the disease as presented at the 2004 Annual Meeting of the *American Psychiatric Association*:

Depression is not in your head. It's in your brain. It is now seen as a neurodegenerative disorder, associated with long-term brain injury. Prolonged depression may result in progressive and cumulative damage to the brain.

The longer you stay depressed, the greater the chances you will not come out of it. Something about depression is toxic.

Depression is best characterized as a syndrome of cellular dysfunction in stress-modulating/mood-regulating brain cells.

Approximately 35 percent of depression is the result of genetic vulnerability. Fully 65 percent of the risk comes from life events. Stress leaves its mark on the brain.

Anxiety increases the risk of subsequent depression fourfold. Eighty-five percent of those with depression have an anxiety disorder first.

Anxiety disorders begin early, in childhood, and affect twice as many girls as boys.

More than 10% of people have some anxiety disorder in any 12-month period, and surveys of freshman college students over the past 40 years indicate that anxiety levels of young people are increasing.

People who experience physical and sexual abuse, parental loss or neglect before puberty are most subject to mood and anxiety disorders later in life. Such events permanently alter the reactivity of the central nervous system, leading to an outsize response to stress.

Those whose depression is linked to adverse events early in life respond better to psychotherapy than to antidepressant drugs.

Experts now see depression as the result of maladaptive interactions between the emotional centers of the brain and the higher "executive" areas, which are responsible for maintaining control in response to stress.

One gene implicated in a depression is the transporter gene for serotonin. A specific variation of the gene seems to predispose people to anxiety-related personality traits, aggression and hyper-excitability of emotional regions of the brain in response to emotionally significant stimuli.

Persons with major depression and panic symptoms have a lower rate of response to treatment than other persons, it takes longer for them to respond, and they are most likely to experience residual symptoms despite treatment.

Depression feeds itself. If you have one depressive episode you have a fifty percent chance of another. If you have two depressive episodes you have a seventy percent chance of another.

Major depressive disorder is more common among white Americans (10.4%) than among African Americans (7.5%) or

Mexican-Americans (8%). But low-grade depression, or dysthymic disorder, is more common among blacks (7.5%) and Mexican-Americans (7.4%) than among whites (5.7%)

Between 1990 and 2001, the number of children diagnosed with depression increased 2.4-fold, from 12.9 per 1,000 children and adolescents to 31.1. The percent of patients prescribed an antidepressant increased from 44.4% to 59.3%. In 1990, 207% of such children received an SSRI; 39.7% did in 2001.

Substance abuse is the rule, not the exception, in bipolar disorder.

Alcoholism is far more common in persons with bipolar disorder (up to sixty percent prevalence rates have been reported) than among persons with unipolar depression (16.5% or the general population (13.8%). Both alcoholism and bipolar disorder are marked by impulsivity.

Bipolar disorder is typically misdiagnosed. Some research shows that the condition is diagnosed correctly in only 20 percent of cases.

Bipolar disorder occurs with greater than normal frequency among persons with cluster headaches and those who are subject to migraine headaches.

Even during manic episodes, those who suffer from bipolar disorder have the same negative thought patterns and core beliefs about the self that are seen in persons with major depression. The findings suggest that cognitive psychotherapy may benefit bipolar patient as well as persons with major depression.

Children of a parent with bipolar disorder are themselves at increased risk for any of a number of psychiatric disorders, from unipolar depression to substance abuse.

Depressed persons with a history of alcohol abuse appear to be at increased risk of suicide, even if they are not currently abusing alcohol.

Anger attacks in depression appear to reflect vascular disease. Brain imaging studies show a higher incidence of lesions in

the white matter among those with depression who experience anger attacks.

Physical inactivity is a risk factor for major depression among
adolescents. Low levels of vigorous exercise and high levels of
sedentary activities constitute independent risk factors for
developing depression over the next year.

Cigarette smoking is far more prevalent among those with
psychiatric disorders than among the general population. In
one survey, nearly fifty percent of bipolar outpatients had a
history of smoking, thirty-five percent were current smokers.

One of the many neurobiological changes that occurs in
depression is decreased ability to generate nerve growth, likely
the toxic effect of over activity of the stress response system.
The lack of nerve growth may account for the inflexibility of
thought processes and memory problems that accompany
depression.

Pregnancy does not protect against occurrence or relapse of
mood disorders. Six percent of pregnant women suffer from
major depression.

In over 50% of cases, the symptoms of postpartum depression
actually begin during pregnancy.

One of two women with major depression during pregnancy
will still suffer from depressive and/or anxiety disorders six
months postpartum.

Maternal depression during pregnancy has significant developmental effects on infants. Infants of depressed moms have
poorer orientation skills, decreased muscle tone, lower activity
levels. It also has negative effects on temperament.

Given the emerging risks of new or recurrent maternal depression on infants, it is not necessary sound advice for women to
discontinue medications in the event of pregnancy.

Acting as a caregiver is psychically demanding. In one study
of older persons caring for a family member who had suffered
a stroke, fully thirty percent developed depression.

Most persons with bipolar disorder also have at least one other psychiatric condition and take multiple psychoactive drugs.

A large-scale clinical trial of the anti-mania drug quetiapine shows that it is also effective against the depressive symptoms of bipolar disorder. The new trials suggest that quetiapine may work solo, simplifying treatment for a disorder that normally involves the use of multiple agents. The drug also improved a broad range of anxiety and mood symptoms associated with bipolar depression.

Depression is not only the most pervasive feature of bipolar disorder but it has been particularly resistant to treatment. It is also associated with suicide attempts.

From 50% to 80% people with major depression experience problems of diminished libido and arousal.

Sexual problems are also prominent side effects of antidepressant drugs. The sexual side effects of the serotonin reuptake inhibiting drugs (SSRIs) may diminish more than sexual drive and performance. They may jeopardize the impetus to fall in love, stay in love or get out of a destructive relationship.

Men are most likely to have problems with desire and orgasm. Women are more likely to have problems with arousal.

Studies show that the combination of drug therapy and psychotherapy is often most effective against depression; delivering the psychotherapy after there has been some response to medication may prove most effective.

Among the emerging ways to enhance the effectiveness of and to speed response to current antidepressant and anti-anxiety medication is the use of so-called atypical antipsychotic agents as adjuncts; these drugs are commonly used to treat bipolar disorder and schizophrenia.

Depression most often produces physical as well as psychological symptoms, and frequently presents as pain in the absence of physical illness.

Persons with major depression are four times more likely to have chronic pain than those without depression.

On average, pain precedes depression by three to five years. One way pain may lead to depression is by disrupting sleep.

The present of pain symptoms predicts poor response to standard antidepressant drug treatment.

Chronically depressed women are most likely to experience somatic symptoms of depression.

By itself, pain multiples the risk of depression approximately fourfold.

Whether pain leads to depression or depression leads to pain is not clear. There are common pathways of neurotransmitters that may explain the overlap.

Pain accompanies anxiety, too, even in the absence of depression.

Adults with attention-deficit disorder have nearly triple the risk of suffering from major depression as well. They have more than five times the risk of bipolar disorder.

Testosterone levels naturally decline in aging men, but the hormone does not seem to play a role in major depression. Decreasing hormone levels may play a role in low-grade depression known as dysthymia, involving symptoms like low libido and fatigue.

Testosterone supplements do not work as a treatment for major depression: Small doses may slightly increase sex drive. Large doses have erratic effects, making some men euphoric and some men angry and irritable.

Sex hormones are known to affect brain functioning. The risk of depression for women transitioning to menopause is higher than normal. The Harvard Study of Moods and Cycles found that women who had never before been depressed were three times more likely to become depressed during the transition; women who had intense hot flashes and other symptoms had six times the risk. Both estrogen replacement therapy and standard antidepressants helped improve mood in menopausal women.

The same study also found that women with heavy menstrual flow or irregular periods are more likely to suffer from depression.

Depression and insomnia are closely linked: More than three-quarters of people with bipolar disorder have insomnia, and sleep difficulties are the single best predictor of episodes of mania in people with this form of depression.

Medical illness is a risk factor for major depressive disorder. While antidepressants are effective, they are less so in people with both depression and physical illness.

The most common reason for discontinuation of antidepressant medication is side effects. Such complaints as gastrointestinal disturbance, agitation and headache often begin with initiation of treatment.

Sexual dysfunction, sleep disturbance, weight gain and cognitive blunting may begin early in treatment and persist after remission.

Sex hormones such as estrogen and progesterone are known to modulate brain function. The abrupt changes in estrogen and progesterone may underlie development of mood disturbances around menopause.

Unipolar major depression is the second leading cause of medical disability in the United States for women, just after heart disease. For men, it is the tenth leading cause of medical disability.

The evidence is stacking up that dramatic changes in the American diet in the past 100 years affect nutritional elements that are critical to nervous system function and thus may play a significant role in major mental health problems. These include fatty acids, B vitamins, antioxidants and chromium. Nutrients are chemicals that affect genes and can switch them on and off.

Depression is associated with shrinkage of the brain, most notably in the hippocampus, a region crucial to memory and other cognitive functions. The effects may be reversible-if depression is treated in time

In addition, another region of the brain, the amygdala, often referred to as the fear center, grows larger.

The brain changes seen in major depression have also been found in persons with bipolar disorder: decreased size of the hippocampus, and increase in the amygdala. The more symptoms of depression patients experience, the greater the brain changes.

All antidepressant drugs work by turning on nerve growth in the brain. Neurogenesis is essential for modulation of feelings.

Exercise also stimulates the growth of new neurons, which may explain why studies show it is an effective treatment for even moderate to severe depression.

The weight gain associated with anti-depressant drugs may represent the body's attempt to elevate blood sugar and force glucose into the brain as a way to fuel the high metabolic demands of neurogenesis.

Psychotherapy and antidepressant drugs both produce measurable—but different—effects on the brain.

Psychotherapy works against depression from the top down, providing cognitive tools that patients can use to interrupt and redirect emotionally relevant stimuli coming through the fear center and other parts of the brain.

The drugs most commonly used against depressions, the SSRIs, may not be effective against pain symptoms even if they alleviate depression.

Evidence suggest that antidepressants that act on levels of norepinephrine as well as on serotonin-so-called dual-reuptake inhibitors-may be more effective in treating depression accompanied by physical symptoms such as pain.

At least thirty percent of patients with depression do not respond to a first course of treatment with SSRI antidepressants.

Only about thirty-five to forty percent of patients achieve full remission after a 6- to 8-week course of antidepressant drug treatment, but increasingly full remission is recognized as necessary for full return to function as well as prevention of relapse.

A new double-blind study shows that the omega-3 fatty acid DHA (docosahexaenoic acid) may be an effective treatment for depression. However, more is not always better. DHA appears to work best at the dose of 1 gram a day. Higher amounts may result in an "overcorrection effect" on fatty acid balance.

Symptoms such as fatigue and sleep problems are most likely to persist after treatment with antidepressant drugs. Some studies show that addition of the drug modafinil may be helpful; a stimulant used to combat sleepiness and improve alertness, it also enhances mood and memory.

The stimulant modafinil may be most useful as adjunctive therapy in persons with so-called atypical depression. Despite the name, atypical depression is an especially common form of the disorder, marked by fatigue, sleepiness and carbohydrate craving often leading to significant weight gain.

Women with bipolar disorder who are treated with anti-seizure medications may be at increased risk for development of osteoporosis.

Patients receiving SSRIs who remain on drug therapy for more than 90 days incur lower annual medical costs than patients who discontinue medication.

appendix e

NEW BRAIN STIMULATION THERAPIES FOR DEPRESSION*

Jerrold F. Rosenbaum, MD and Amy E. Judy

Introduction

Although the use of convulsive therapies such as electroconvulsive therapy (ECT) has been stigmatized over the years by harsh images, their antidepressant efficacy is not questioned.[1,2] Seizures induced by a number of means — electrical, chemical, and magnetic — have all been associated with subsequently improved mood, leading to the conclusion that the seizure itself ameliorates symptoms of depression.[1] However, research presented at the American Psychiatric Association 2004 Annual Meeting in New York, NY suggests that seizures may not be requisite to the antidepressant effects of ECT, and further proposes that several types of brain stimulation that are not based on the induction of generalized convulsions may be efficacious treatments for depression. Among these new therapies are transcranial magnetic stimulation (TMS) and vagus nerve stimulation (VNS).

169

Harold Sackeim, PhD and colleagues,[3] at the New York Psychiatric Institute, have shown that by varying electrode placement and/or the current delivered during ECT treatment, seizures can be induced that do not lessen symptoms of depression. This finding supports the idea that the stimulation site, rather than the seizure, may be more critical to the therapeutic effects of ECT than was originally believed. Imaging studies that examine brain activity following ECT provide further evidence in favor of the site-not-seizure hypothesis, by showing that spatially distinct areas of the brain are affected when electrode placement and/or current intensity of the treatment is varied.[2] ECT is known to result in an overall diminution of activity in the brain; specifically, the prefrontal cortex shows a marked reduction in metabolism following ECT.[4] Stimulation paradigms that cause reductions in prefrontal cortex activity have been related to decreases in depressive symptoms, while interventions that also correlate with decreased activity in the temporal cortex are associated with greater cognitive side effects, including retrograde amnesia and slowed reaction times. The discordance in the effects of ECT dependent upon site of stimulation suggests that therapies based on more selective targeting of stimulation may increase efficacy and limit side effects.

Transcranial Magnetic Stimulation

TMS relies on an intense magnetic field to depolarize neurons and generate pulses of electrical activity similar to those observed with ECT. But unlike ECT, the waves do not result in generalized seizure activity.[5] The magnetic field applied in TMS is generated by movement of current around a specially designed coil, located in a hand-held device positioned directly above the subject's skull. The rapid jump from the normal field exerted by the earth to a magnetic field roughly 20,000 times more intense causes neuronal depolarization — not the intensity of the field itself. This mechanism of action may explain what researchers such as Ziad Nahas, MD,[6] of the Medical University of South Carolina, cite as one of the crucial differences between TMS therapy and ECT; changes in brain activity that occur with TMS resemble those changes induced by voluntary motor actions.[7]

But what make TMS most promising are the inherent qualities of magnetic field, which lend themselves to better control and more precise application. The magnetic waves of TMS pass through bone and tissue relatively undiminished, delivering a virtual beam of intense stimulation to the desired location.[5] Electric current, Dr Nahas explained, is shunted off in various directions by the skull.[6] The high-insulation capacity of bone defers much energy to far-reaching areas of the cortex and only allows a limited amount through to the tissue immediately beneath the point of stimulation. Somewhat paradoxically, the magnetic field of TMS is also controlled in its restricted depth of penetration. Magnetic field intensity falls off steeply as a function of distance,[8] only allowing direct stimulation to levels about 2 cm below the skull. Though this shallow depth in some ways limits the applicability of TMS for deep-brain stimulation, it dramatically increases the ability of clinicians to target a specific region of effect.

A number of studies have shown TMS to cause alterations in brain metabolic activity and neurochemistry that mimic other antidepressant therapies. TMS of the prefrontal cortex has been associated with dopamine release in the ipsilateral caudate,[9] and studies of TMS in rats have also shown that the magnetic stimulation induces an anxiolytic effect and rebalances serotonin in the brain.[10] Despite the number of animal studies that have found TMS superior to sham treatment, Dr. Nahas commented that animal studies have proven challenging, as the ratio of the size of the TMS device to the rat brain is far greater than the ratio of the same device to a human brain. Rats therefore receive much more than just prefrontal cortex stimulation, and so these studies, positive and negative, ought to be regarded with caution.

While the future of TMS appears promising, clinical trials of the therapy are in the earliest stages and have produced mixed results. TMS has demonstrated antidepressant effects in some short trials and as concluded from some large-scale meta-analyses. One of the most favorable sham-control studies looked at patients diagnosed with major depression (N = 20) and found a 45% response rate (HRS-D reduction >/= 50%) in subjects after 10 days of TMS therapy, with no patients responding to sham treatment.[11] Other studies have shown efficacy of TMS over sham in the treatment of acute depression,[12] but negative data have also been reported for MDD.[13] A recent meta-analysis by Gershon and colleagues[14] concluded that longer stimulation and higher intensity stimulation both increase effect sizes of TMS therapy, which has encouraged ongoing research into TMS therapy despite the publication of some negative trials. Additionally, the comparable efficacy of TMS to ECT has been questioned. One study looking at 40 depressed subjects receiving TMS or ECT revealed no significant difference in response between the groups after 20 days of treatment, and actually found superior response to ECT in psychotically depressed patients.[15] However, when paired with a favorable side-effect profile, TMS may still pose benefits despite only equivalent (not superior) efficacy compared with ECT.

Additionally, Dr. Nahas explained that some of the negative trials may be attributed to a lack of foresight in study design rather than deficient efficacy of TMS. Atrophy of the brain, a common phenomenon in geriatric patients, may reduce effect sizes by increasing the distance over which the magnetic field must travel. As previously noted, the intensity of magnetic fields falls off steeply with increases in distance, and an atrophied brain creates more distance from the skull than observed in a "normal" brain. Studies have addressed atrophy by increasing stimulation intensity in older patients, and these studies have elicited positive outcomes from non-responders of previous studies that did not address the possible effects of atrophy.[8] TMS may be a fruitful therapy for subgroups of depressed patients, but perhaps not all. Research examining possible predictors of response may eventually identify the subgroups of depressed patients for which TMS is and is not appropriate.

Although TMS is a therapy intended to provide seizure-free

stimulation, its safety has not been completely established. In the lab of Dr. Nahas, unintended seizures have been induced by TMS therapy in rare instances — he recalls 9 carefully documented cases. In these cases, Nahas and colleagues determined that the applied magnetic fields either increased in intensity too rapidly or were applied for too long. These instances serve to emphasize the need for established treatment parameters that provide the highest efficacy while limiting adverse events.

Vagus Nerve Stimulation

VNS is another seizure-free, stimulation-based therapy currently being explored for the treatment of depression. VNS has been approved for the treatment of epilepsy in the United States since 1997, and it has been indicated for treatment-resistant depression and treatment-intolerant depression in the European Union and Canada since 2001. However, it is still awaiting US Food and Drug Administration approval for the treatment of unipolar and/or bipolar depression in the United States. In VNS therapy, a mild electrical pulse is applied to the left vagus nerve via an implantable device positioned under the skin of the neck during an outpatient surgery. The device is programmed to automatically stimulate the afferent fibers of the vagus nerve for 30 seconds every 5 minutes. This stimulation occurs 24 hours a day, 7 days a week, and lasts for as long as the life of the battery within the implant — generally about 10 years.

Lauren Marangell, MD,[16] of Baylor University in Texas, described the current evidence for VNS therapy in the treatment of depression. The safety of VNS has been well established, and Marangell estimated that some 22,000 patients worldwide with implanted VNS devices are being treated for epilepsy. It is thought that VNS elicits its antidepressant effects indirectly; the vagus nerve stimulates the nucleus of the solitary tract through direct afferent connection, and this area, in turn, stimulates limbic structures, the same structures associated with animal models of depression. Studies have also shown that VNS increases turnover rates in a number of neurotransmitters implicated in depression, including serotonin, norepinephrine, and dopamine.[15,17]

Initial clinical trials of VNS therapy for depression have reported acute antidepressant responses and sustained or improved long-term benefit. An open-label trial of the therapy tracked 60 subjects over an 8-week, fixed-dose period.[18,19] The subjects were considered very treatment resistant at baseline (mean Hamilton Rating Scale for Depression [HRSD$_{28}$] 36.8), and they had a mean length of current depressive episode of 9.9 years. Notably, 66% of the subjects had experienced ECT treatment during the current depressive episode. At 3 months, 31% of subjects showed response (reduced HRSD$_{28}$ >/= 50), and 15% of responders were in remission (HRSD$_{28}$ </= 10). Follow-up at 1 year found an increase in response (45% response rate, 27% remission) and a decrease in reported adverse events.

A subsequent study, which was blinded and placebo-controlled, excluded subjects (n = 222) considered "extremely treatment resistant" based on large numbers of previous treatment failures, but subjects were considered similarly ill (mean HRSD$_{24}$ = 27.9). Only 36% had received ECT during the current depressive episode. The study mainly examined VNS in unipolar depression, though 10% of study subjects were actually diagnosed with bipolar depression. The placebo-controlled trial demonstrated a 15% response rate to VNS (HRSD$_{24}$ reduction), with 10% of sham-control subjects responding. Long-term follow-up at 12 months found 29.8% response rate, with 17.1% of subjects in full remission (reduction in HRSD$_{24}$). Though these response rates were not statistically significant when compared with the sham-control response rates, examination of IDS-SR scores showed significance on some measures (21.7% response to VNS, 15% response to sham). Response and remission rates identified in the previous study held steady at 2 years (44% response, 22% remission).[20]

Dr. Marangell stressed an additional feature of VNS therapy — a built in adherence rate. At 12 months, 90% of subjects were still utilizing their VNS devices. Of those subjects who chose not to continue with VNS treatment, 3.0% dropped out due to adverse events, and 4.6% stopped treatment citing insufficient efficacy. Like any treatment, though, VNS is not without its side effects, but compared with ECT and pharmacologic interventions, these effects are mild. Cough, voice alteration, and tingling in the region around the implanted device are the most common complaints.[19] These side effects decrease with time and have been found to be highly amenable to changes in device programming. And unlike ECT and other seizure-based therapies, VNS has not been associated with any cognitive side effects.[21]

Clinical trials into the use of VNS as a therapy for unipolar and bipolar depression are ongoing, and current and past studies have based device settings of stimulation intensity and duration on optimal treatment for epilepsy. It is not yet known what ideal settings for treatment of depression may turn out to be, and it is possible that the side effects of VNS may be decreased when optimal settings are identified.

Conclusion

More than 70 years after the first therapeutic application of electrically induced seizures, the field of brain stimulation therapies appears ready for innovation. Though widely acknowledged as "the most effective antidepressant" available to clinicians today, the impressive efficacy of ECT is overshadowed by its side effect profile and stigmatization, in the media and elsewhere. Today, ECT has been refined; application is more precise, anesthesia is the norm, and negative side effects have been significantly reduced. But despite these advances, ECT is still an unacceptable option for many, even the most severely ill. Hence, new stimulation therapies like VNS and TMS, which are not based on seizure induction but may show similarly high efficacy without such a tremendous side effect burden, are very desirable indeed.

References
1. Fink M. Convulsive therapy: a review of the first 55 years. J Affect Disord. 2001;63:1-15. Abstract
2. Sackeim HA, Prudic J, Devanand DP, et al. A prospective, randomized, double-blind comparison of bilateral and right unilateral

electroconvulsive therapy at different stimulus intensities. Arch Gen Psychiatry. 2000;57:425-434. Abstract

3. Sackeim HA. Central issues regarding the mechanisms of action of electroconvulsive therapy: directions for future research. Psychopharmacol Bull. 1994;30:281-308. Abstract

4. Nobler MS, Oquendo MA, Kegeles LS, et al. Decreased regional brain metabolism after ECT. Am J Psychiatry. 2001;158:305-308. Abstract

5. George MS, Nahas Z, Kozol FA, et al. Mechanisms and the current state of transcranial magnetic stimulation. CNS Spectr. 2003;8:496-514. Abstract

6. Nahas ZH, Kozel AF, Mishory A, et al. Repeated prefrontal repetitive transcranial magnetic stimulation as an antidepressant: an update. Program and abstracts of the American Psychiatric Association 2004 Annual Meeting; May 1-6, 2004; New York, NY. Symposium 1C.

7. Bohning DE, Shastri A, McGavin L, et al. Motor cortex brain activity induced by 1-Hz transcranial magnetic stimulation is similar in location and level to that for volitional movement. Invest Radiol. 2000;35:676-683. Abstract

8. Nahas Z, Teneback CC, Kozel A, et al. Brain effects of TMS delivered over prefrontal cortex in depressed adults: role of stimulation frequency and coil-cortex distance. J Neuropsychiatry Clin Neurosci. 2001;13:459-470. Abstract

9. Strafella AP, Paus T, Barrett J, Dagher A. Repetitive transcranial magnetic stimulation of the human prefrontal cortex induces dopamine release in the caudate nucleus. J Neurosci. 2001;21:RC157.

10. Kanno M, Matsumoto M, Togashi H, Yoshioka M, Mano Y. Effects of repetitive transcranial magnetic stimulation on behavioral and neurochemical changes in rats during an elevated plus-maze test. J Neurol Sci. 2003;211:5-14. Abstract

11. Little JT, Kimbrell TA, Wassermann EM, et al. Cognitive effects of 1- and 20-hertz repetitive transcranial magnetic stimulation in depression: preliminary report. Neuropsychiatry Neuropsychol Behav Neurol. 2000;13:119-124. Abstract

12. Fitzgerald PB, Brown TL, Marston NA, Daskalakis ZJ, De Castella A, Kulkarni J. Transcranial magnetic stimulation in the treatment of depression: a double-blind, placebo-controlled trial. Arch Gen Psychiatry. 2003;60:1002-1008. Abstract

13. Loo CK, Mitchell PB, Croker VM, et al. Double-blind controlled investigation of bilateral prefrontal transcranial magnetic stimulation for the treatment of resistant major depression [see comment]. Psychol Med. 2003;33:33-40. Abstract

14. Gershon AA, Dannon PN, Grunhaus L. Transcranial magnetic stimulation in the treatment of depression. Am J Psychiatry. 2003;160:835-845. Abstract

15. Grunhaus L, Dannon PN, Schreiber S, et al. Repetitive transcranial magnetic stimulation is as effective as electroconvulsive therapy in the treatment of nondelusional major depressive disorder: an open study. Biol Psychiatry. 2000;47:314-324. Abstract

16. Marangell L. The use of vagus nerve stimulation (VNS) in the long-term treatment of mood disorders. Program and abstracts of the American Psychiatric Association 2004 Annual Meeting; May 1-6, 2004; New York, NY. Symposium 1D.

17. Ben-Menachem E, Hamberger A, Hedner T, et al. Effects of vagus nerve stimulation on amino acids and other metabolites in the CSF of patients with partial seizures. Epilepsy Res. 1995;20:221-227. Abstract

18. Sackeim HA, Rush AJ, George MS, et al. Vagus nerve stimulation (VNS) for treatment-resistant depression: efficacy, side effects, and predictors of outcome. Neuropsychopharmacology. 2001;25:713-728. Abstract

19. Marangell LB, Rush AJ, George MS, et al. Vagus nerve stimulation (VNS) for major depressive episodes: one year outcomes. Biol Psychiatry. 2002;51:280-287. Abstract

20. George MS, Rush AJ, Sackeim HA, Marangell LB. Vagus nerve stimulation (VNS): utility in neuropsychiatric disorders. Int J Neuropsychopharmacol. 2003;6:73-83. Abstract

21. Sackeim HA, Keilp JG, Rush AJ, et al. The effects of vagus nerve stimulation on cognitive performance in patients with treatment-resistant depression. Neuropsychiatry Neuropsychol Behav Neurol. 2001;14:53-62. Abstract

Update on TMS

"A deficit of TMS is that it is very labor intensive spread over several weeks, while the therapeutic effects seem to last only a few days to a few weeks," according to an article published in *Scientific American MIND*, Summer 2005.

"TMS is still in an experimental stage, however. Only a few trials, involving a small number of test subjects, have been published. The types of people, brain locations, coil configurations, and magnetic fields strengths and frequencies have varied considerably," according to Mark George, MD. A metastudy of depression trials also concluded that there was no strong evidence of benefit.

O

appendix f

THE RELATIONSHIP BETWEEN DEPRESSION AND PHYSICAL SYMPTOMS*

Thomas A. M. Kramer, MD

Introduction

This symposium looked at the relationship between depression and physical symptomatology not usually considered in depression diagnosis, such as pain or gastrointestinal dysfunction. Presenters addressed the common incidence of these co-occurrences, the neurochemical systems involved as illustrated through neuroimaging, some information about the specific neuroanatomic structures that may be involved, the consideration of gender differences in physical symptoms of depression, and finally a discussion of best practices for achieving remission in depression with physical symptomatology.

Comorbidities

The first speaker was Kurt Kroenke, MD,[1] Professor of Medicine at the Indiana University School of Medicine, Indianapolis, Indiana. He initially made some crucial distinctions for these discussions. He pointed out the difference between medical comorbidities of depression (eg, cardiovascular disease) and physical symptoms that may be symptomatic of depression (eg, chronic pain). He also discussed the distinction between physical symptoms, which is a term used commonly by nonpsychiatric physicians to describe bodily symptoms, and somatic symptoms, which can easily be mistakenly equated with somatoform, implying a different psychiatric etiology. He then revealed some interesting global statistics — of 400 million clinic visits per year for primary care, half are for pain, 30% are for respiratory complaints, and only 20% are for something else. The top 3 complaints are back pain, knee or hip pain, and abdominal pain. One third of the time, physical symptoms are medically unexplained. This number goes up dramatically in patients with comorbid psychiatric disorders: it is almost two thirds for patients with depression and almost half for patients with an anxiety disorder.

The actual number of physical symptoms is also related directly to both the likelihood of them being medically unexplained and the likelihood for psychiatric comorbidities. Even in specialty clinics, this becomes an issue: approximately half of the patients seen in either gastroenterology or neurology clinics, for example, have medically unexplained symptoms. One study he cited looked at how patients with psychiatric disorders, specifically depression, presented in primary care clinics and to what extent their depression was recognized. Those patients who presented with psychological symptomatology were recognized 90% of the time, but those depressed patients who presented with somatic symptoms were only recognized 50% of the time, and if they presented with a medical disorder they were only recognized 20% of the time.[2] He shared data from a World Health Organization study that showed that somatization of depression did not vary by country.[3]

Pain and Depression
He then spoke about the overlap between pain and depres-

sion; pooling multiple studies showed that approximately 60% of depressed patients have pain and 30% of pain patients have depression. Pain symptoms make depression and anxiety disorders considerably more likely, particularly if the symptoms are unexplained. He made the point that physical and psychological symptoms can be both the cause and the consequence of each other. He talked about antidepressants as treatment for pain conditions, and that they all are not equally effective, with tricyclic antidepressants being somewhat more effective than selective serotonin reuptake inhibitors (SSRIs). He showed data that the more severe the pain condition is, the less likely the patient is to respond to treatment, and discussed antidepressants as part of a pain management program including analgesics and psychosocial treatments, specifically cognitive behavioral therapy.[4]

Neuroimaging

Jon-Kar Zubieta, MD, PhD,[5] Associate Professor of Psychiatry and Radiology at the University Of Michigan, Ann Arbor, Michigan, spoke about the increasing amount of data being collected from both animal research and human neuroimaging studies showing that the same or similar neural networks and neurochemical mechanisms seem to be involved with the regulation of physical stress, physical symptoms, and depression. Some of the brain regions that have been implicated in the response to mood symptoms, stress, and painful and noxious stimuli include the anterior cingulate, prefrontal and insular cortex, the amygdala, ventral basal ganglia, and anterior thalamus. These overlaps may help to explain clinical linkages between depression, anxiety, and physical symptomatology. He discussed some of the neurochemical systems involved, such as mu opioid receptor-mediated neurotransmission, and some of the methodology of the investigations, such as functional neuroimaging during hypertonic and isotonic saline infusions. He then described some genetic variability, specifically in the COMT enzyme activity genotype. Finally, he talked about gender differences in these systems and showed some physiological differences potentially mediated by estradiol.

Structural Brain Changes in Depression

The next speaker was Bruce McEwan, PhD,[6] Professor of Neuroendocrinology at The Rockefeller University, New York, NY. He spoke about structural changes in the brain in depression, and specifically discussed 2 structures: the hippocampus and the amygdala. Generally, there seems to be atrophy of the hippocampus and at least initial hypertrophy of the amygdala in depression, but perhaps atrophy later in the disease. The hippocampus, whose primary function appears to be crucial to certain types of learning and memory, has very high levels of adrenal steroid receptors. It displays neurogenesis throughout adult life, but in the presence of stress-induced hyperexcretion of adrenal steroids, this cell growth may be dramatically attenuated. In addition, the excitatory neurotransmitter glutamate also suppresses neurogenesis, and some forms of stress may increase extracellular glutamate levels. Lithium may be protective of this process. While this atrophy of the hippocampus may cause some cognitive impairment, the increase, at least initially, in the volume of the amygdala may cause increased anxiety and aggression. Preliminary evidence shows that these changes are reversible, although the extent to which they are reversible is not clear.

Gender Differences in Depression

Vivien Burt, MD, PhD,[7] Professor of Clinical Psychiatry at the UCLA School of Medicine, Los Angeles, California, spoke about gender issues in the treatment of depression with physical symptoms. She started with some demographics demonstrating the differential burdens of depression between women and men. Depression is the second leading cause of medical disability for women, but the tenth leading cause for men. Depression is more prevalent in every adult age group for women than men. Women are also considerably more likely than men to have physical symptoms outside of the DSM criteria for both depression and anxiety disorders. While "pure" depressions without any other physical symptoms or comorbid anxiety disorders are equally common in women and men, anxious somatic depressions are considerably more common in women. The implication of this is that the difference in prevalence between genders is a function of the increased rate of "somatic depression."

Since there is considerable evidence of overlap of the physiology of pain and mood disorders, the question remains as to whether antidepressants treat both, and probably the reason that many patients do not achieve remission is because painful symptoms are not addressed as a component of the depression. Dr. Burt reviewed both psychosocial variables such as sociocultural disadvantages and increased child rearing burdens, and biological variables such as reproductive related transitions including puberty, premenstrual days, peri- and postpartum, and perimenopause that contribute to depression in women. She then focused in on perimenopausal depression because it is particularly prone to physical symptomatology. A lifetime history of depression and current depression are associated with earlier perimenopause. For some perimenopausal depressed women, this transition can improve mood, and the shorter the perimenopausal transition, the less likely there will be depression.

Recommendations for perimenopausal depression involve psychotherapy and antidepressants, and Dr. Burt recommended dual-acting agents that work via both serotonin and noradrenergic systems. There have been 3 positive studies about the use of estrogen in perimenopausal depression, and these responses take place in the perimenopausal period but not in postmenopausal women, and this improvement is independent of vasomotor symptoms. In the recent study of hormone replacement therapy that found that the sum of risks was greater than the sum of benefits for postmenopausal women, perimenopausal women were not represented. Estrogen therapy may be an option for depressed perimenopausal women. In the treatment of perimenopausal depression and hot flashes, there have been positive studies for venlafaxine, paroxetine, and fluoxetine, and antidepressants should be considered to treat both conditions. Finally, she concluded by saying that remission, not just response, should be the goal of treatment, that physical symptoms are common presentations in depressed patients, particularly women, and the comprehensive treatment of all symptoms may make the difference.

The Future of Treatment

The final speaker and the chair of the symposium was John Greden, MD,[8] Chairman of the Department of Psychiatry at the University of Michigan, Ann Arbor, Michigan. He pointed out that new treatment approaches must emphasize earlier detection, earlier intervention, achievement of remission, prevention of progression, and integration of neurosciences and behavioral sciences. To do this, we must partner with primary care and special care colleagues, screen patients earlier, educate the public better, develop new treatments for remission for patients with physical symptoms, and counteract stigma. He pointed out the difficulty of primary and specialty care clinicians in dealing with depression, citing data that they have approximately 11 minutes in any given visit to do so.

He then spoke about screening high-risk ages and groups, such as late adolescence and early adults, women in reproductive years, adults with medical problems, and people with family history of depression. He demonstrated the University of Michigan's Depression Center Web site as an example. He talked about the first group, patients aged 15 to 24 years, as being important because it is where underdiagnosis often appears as a function of depression being explained away to the developmental stresses involved with that period. He talked about the success of a screening program for depression during pregnancy in both finding untreated depressions and improving the treatment. He then also addressed the issue of finding untreated depression in high-risk groups such as older adults and medically all patients.

He then stressed the importance of education, particularly about the linkage between physical symptoms and depression. He showed some examples from the national media as to how the public is getting better educated and stressed that clinicians need to make these kinds of materials, in the form of magazines and brochures, available in their offices. He reviewed some of the information about neurogenesis presented in previous talks and pointed out that untreated brain diseases and comorbidities are not good for brains.

He then talked about differential therapeutics, and in particular antidepressants. He pointed out that different antidepressants are better or worse for different conditions. For example, SSRIs are much better than tricyclic antidepressants for obsessive-compulsive disorder and premenstrual dysphoric disorder, but dual reuptake blockers (serotonin norepinephrine reuptake inhibitors [SNRIs]) and tricyclics may be better for pain and physical symptoms. He then went on to discuss this last point with some physiological references to pain pathways being mediated by both serotonin and norepinephrine. He speculated that the relatively high percentage of patients with pain and depression who fail to achieve remission may be because they are being treated with less effective SSRIs. He then showed data for 2 SNRIs, venlafaxine and duloxetine, showing their effectiveness. He advocated combining antidepressants and cognitive behavioral therapy by showing some data that demonstrated their combined effectiveness.

Dr. Greden also discussed potential future treatments and illustrated what an ideal antidepressant would be, with higher rates of response, remission, and adherence, lower rates of recurrences, faster onset, and high levels of safety and convenience. He presented list of potential future treatments including repetitive transcranial magnetic stimulation, vagal nerve stimulation, magnetic seizure therapy, deep brain stimulation, corticotroponin-releasing hormone antagonists, triple uptake inhibitors, substance P or neurokinin antagonists, vasopression receptor antagonists, secretin antagonists, cognition activators, brain derived neurotrophic factor promoters, melatonin agonists, and susceptibility alleles. He speculated that the future will involve more genetic screening and pharmacogenomics and that neuroimaging and other studies currently restricted for the most part to research studies will become more common in everyday practice. Finally, he suggested the following changes to our practice to decrease the burden of depression with physical symptoms: earlier diagnosis and intervention, more attention to family history, reintroduction of neurobiological variables, more sensible treatment selection and augmentation strategies, promotion of sleep hygiene and exercise, and better total health care, similar to what cardiologists have been promoting with good result.

References

1. Kroenke K. Underdetection and inadequate treatment of physical symptoms of depression: the real barriers to remission. Program and abstracts of the American Psychiatric Association 2004 Annual Meeting; May 1-6, 2004; New York, NY. Symposium 19A.
2. Bijl D, van Marwijk HW, de Haan M, van Tilburg W, Beekman AJ. Effectiveness of disease management programmes for recognition, diagnosis and treatment of depression in primary care. Eur J Gen Pract. 2004;10:6-12. Abstract
3. Gureje O, Simon GE, Ustun TB, Goldberg DP. Somatization in cross-cultural perspective: a World Health Organization study in primary care. Am J Psychiatry. 1997;154:989-995. Abstract
4. Tumlin TR, Kvaal S. Psychotherapeutic issues encountered in the psychotherapy of chronic pain patients. Curr Pain Headache Rep. 2004;8:125-129. Abstract
5. Zubieta J. Neurochemical systems interfacing physical and emotional stressors. Program and abstracts of the American Psychiatric Association 2004 Annual Meeting; May 1-6, 2004; New York, NY. Symposium 19A.
6. McEwen BS. Stress effects on the hippocampus: relevance to depression. Program and abstracts of the American Psychiatric Association 2004 Annual Meeting; May 1-6, 2004; New York, NY. Symposium 19C.
7. Burt VK. Gender considerations in the treatment of physical symptoms of depression. Program and abstracts of the American Psychiatric Association 2004 Annual Meeting; May 1-6, 2004; New York, NY. Symposium 19D.
8. Greden JF. Best practices for achieving remission in depression with physical symptoms: current and future trends. Program and abstracts of the American Psychiatric Association 2004 Annual Meeting; May 1-6, 2004; New York, NY. Symposium 19E.

○
appendix g

MENTAL HEALTH RESOURCES AND ADVOCACY

Mental Health Resources

Depression and Bipolar Support Alliance (DBSA)
730 N. Franklin Street, Suite 501
Chicago, Illinois 60610-7224 USA
Phone: 800-826-3632 (toll-free)
http://www.dbsalliance.org/

Mental Health Resource Center
Phone: 800-969-NMHA

National Alliance for Research on Schizophrenia and
Depression (NARSAD)
60 Cutter Mill Road, Suite 404
Great Neck, New York 11021
Phone: 516 829-0091 or 1-800-829-8289
Fax: 516 487-6930
info@narsad.org

National Alliance for the Mentally Ill (NAMI)
Colonial Place Three
2107 Wilson Blvd., Suite 300
Arlington, VA 22201-3042
Phone: 1-800-950-NAMI (6264)
http://www.nami.org/

National Hopeline Network (1-800-SUICIDE)
2001 North Beauregard Street, 12 Floor
Alexandria, Virginia 22311
Phone: (703) 837-3364
E-Mail: Info@Hopeline.com
http://www.hopeline.com/

National Institute of Mental Health (NIMH)
Public Information and Communications Branch
6001 Executive Boulevard, Room 8184, MSC 9663
Bethesda, MD 20892-9663
Phone: 301-443-4513 (local) or 1-866-615-6464 (toll-free)
E-mail: nimhinfo@nih.gov

National Mental Health Association
2001 N. Beauregard Street, 12th Floor
Alexandria, VA 22311
Phone: 703-684-7722
Fax: 703-684-5968

Depression and Related Affective Disorders Association (DRADA)
2330 West Joppa Rd., Suite 100
Lutherville, MD 21093
Phone: 410-583-2919
E-mail: drada@jhmi.edu
http://www.drada.org/

Charles E. Donovan, III

September 30,2003

The Honorable William Clay
House of Representatives
Washington, DC 20515

Dear Representative Clay,

I am writing to urge Congress to take up and pass now the Senator Paul Wellstone Mental Health Equitable Treatment Act, legislation to end blatant and widespread discrimination against people with mental illness.

Mental illness is the second leading cause of disability and premature mortality in the United States. Yet every day families with "good health coverage" discover that their loved ones who have mental illnesses cannot get needed care because their insurance sets strict limits on mental health treatment - like ending further coverage after a limited number of treatment sessions - but imposes no such limits on treating any other illness.

These practices are not only unfair, they're irrational. Mental illnesses are reliably diagnosed and for virtually every mental disorder, there is a range of treatments and services that have been shown to be effective.

Health insurers who erect these barriers to medically necessary mental health treatment inflict enormous harm on American families...and on our economy. These discriminatory practices - which are applied only to mental disorders - cause illnesses to go untreated and worsen. Tragically, this lack of care leads all too often to unemployment, broken homes, school failure, and even suicide. Untreated mental illness also costs our economy about $80 billion each year -- in lost productivity, sick leave, and unemployment.

American families need a solution NOW. The solution is bipartisan legislation that would require simple parity between mental health benefits and the benefits provided to treat any other illness or injury. This simple, fair step will save lives and families.

As studies have shown, mental health parity legislation will not lead to a significant increase in insurance premiums or in the number of uninsured Americans. But the costs of NOT enacting parity are high, and will fall most heavily on taxpayer-funded public programs, our economy, and the well-being of American families and their communities.

Please make passage of a strong mental health parity bill a top priority before Congress adjourns this year.

Sincerely,

Charles E. Donovan, III

Charles E. Donovan, III

Via Fax

January 19, 2004

The Honorable Bill Frist,M.D.
Dirksen Senate Office Building
Washington, D.C. 20510

Re: The World Health Care Congress-January 25th-27th, 2004

Dear Senator Frist,

I read in today's Wall Street Journal, that you are listed as one of the
speakers scheduled to give a "Visionary Address" at this ground break-
ing U.S. Leadership Forum to Transform Health Care Costs and Quality.

I would like to urge you to speak out against the blatant and widespread discrimination against people with mental illness. Health
insurers, including Medicare, discriminate reimbursement levels against
mental illnesses versus any other type of illness.

Untreated mental illness costs the economy $80 billion a year and
unquantifiable human suffering.

As you speak in front of our country's health care leaders, please
make a top priority, the passage of a strong mental health parity bill
by Congress.

Sincerely,

Charles E. Donovan

O
appendix h

HAMILTON RATING SCALE FOR DEPRESSION

The Hamilton Rating Scale for Depression (HRSD), also known as HAM-D, instrument is designed to be used only on patients already diagnosed as suffering from affective disorder of the depressive type. It is used for quantifying the results of an interview and its value depends entirely on the skill of the interviewer in eliciting the necessary information. The scale contains seventeen variables measured on either a five-point or a three-point rating scale, the latter being used where quantification of the variable is either difficult or impossible. Among the variables are: depressed mood, suicide, work and loss of interest, retardation, agitation, gastrointestinal symptoms, general somatic symptoms, hypochondriasis, loss of insight, and loss of weight.

Scoring the Hamilton Depression Rating Scale (HDRS)

The total HDRS score provides an indication of the level of a patient's depression and, over time, provides a valuable guide to a patient's progress. In general, the higher the total score, the more severe is the depression. While it is not realistic to categorically assign a specific level of depression to a specific HDRS score, it is possible to give the following general guidelines:

HDRS Score: Level of depression:
10 - 13   Mild
13 - 17   Mild to Moderate
> 17   Moderate to severe

The seventeen questions are designed to be administered by a healthcare professional and are used to rate the severity of depression in patients already diagnosed as depressed.

Hamilton Rating Scale for Depression

This questionnaire cannot replace an evaluation by a professional, but it can familiarize you with the symptoms of depression and give you an idea if you may meet the diagnostic criteria for clinical depression.

Appropriate for: Patients diagnosed with depression

Administered by: Physician or trained raters

Time to complete: 30 minutes

Summary: HRSD/HAM-D is a 17-item observer-rated scale to assess the presence and severity of depressive states where anxiety-related symptoms are prevalent and no other depressive symptoms are present.

9 items are scored 0-4, whereas the further 8 are scored 0-2, as these represent variables that do not lend themselves to quantitative rating (0=absent; 1=doubtful or slight; 2=mild; 3=moderate; 4=severe. 0=absent; 1=doubtful or slight; 2=clearly present).

A score of 10 is generally regarded as indicative of a diagnosis of depression.

Conducted in semi-structured interview carried out by trained a clinician.

Benefits of HRSD
- Widely used: HRSD and HAM-D are the most widely used instruments for clinical assessment of depressive symptoms.
- Well-validated: The tool was developed in 1960 and since that time has been widely evaluated and established as a highly reliable and valid assessment tool.
- 'Gold'-standard of depression rating scales.
- Frequently used in studies as an anchor with which to compare newer instruments.

To rate the severity of depression in patients who are already diagnosed as depressed, clinicians administer this questionnaire. The higher the score, the more severe the depression.

For each item, write the correct number on the line next to the item. (Only one response per item)

1. DEPRESSED MOOD (Sadness, hopeless, helpless, worthless)
   0= Absent
   1= These feeling states indicated only on questioning
   2= These feeling states spontaneously reported verbally
   3= Communicates feeling states non-verbally-i.e., through facial expression, posture, voice, and tendency to weep
   4= Patient reports VIRTUALLY ONLY these feeling states in his spontaneous verbal and nonverbal communication

2. FEELINGS OF GUILT
   0= Absent
   1= Self-reproach, feels he has let people down
   2= Ideas of guilt or rumination over past errors or sinful deeds
   3= Present illness is a punishment. Delusions of guilt
   4= Hears accusatory or denunciatory voices and/or experiences threatening visual hallucinations

3. SUICIDE
0= Absent
1= Feels life is not worth living
2= Wishes he were dead or any thoughts of possible death to self
3= Suicidal ideas or gesture
4= Attempts at suicide (any serious attempt rates 4)

4. INSOMNIA EARLY
0= No difficulty falling asleep
1= Complains of occasional difficulty falling asleep-i.e., more than 1/2 hour
2= Complains of nightly difficulty falling asleep

5. INSOMNIA MIDDLE
0= No difficulty
1= Patient complains of being restless and disturbed during the night
2= Waking during the night-any getting out of bed rates 2 (except for purposes of voiding)

7. INSOMNIA LATE
0= No difficulty
1= Waking in early hours of the morning but goes back to sleep 2= Unable to fall asleep again if he gets out of bed

8. WORK AND ACTIVITIES
0= No difficulty
1= Thoughts and feelings of incapacity, fatigue or weakness related to activities; work or hobbies
2= Loss of interest in activity; hobbies or work-either directly reported by patient, or indirect in listlessness, indecision and vacillation (feels he has to push self to work or activities)
3= Decrease in actual time spent in activities or decrease in productivity
4= Stopped working because of present illness

9. RETARDATION: PSYCHOMOTOR (Slowness of thought and speech; impaired ability to concentrate; decreased motor activity)
0= Normal speech and thought
1= Slight retardation at interview
2= Obvious retardation at interview
3= Interview difficult
4= Complete stupor

10. AGITATION
0= None
1= Fidgetiness
2= Playing with hands, hair, etc.
3= Moving about, can't sit still
4= Hand wringing, nail biting, hair-pulling, biting of lips

11. ANXIETY (PSYCHOLOGICAL)
0= No difficulty
1= Subjective tension and irritability
2= Worrying about minor matters
3= Apprehensive attitude apparent in face or speech 4= Fears expressed without questioning

11. ANXIETY SOMATIC: Physiological concomitants of anxiety, (i.e., effects of autonomic overactivity, "butterflies," indigestion, stomach cramps, belching, diarrhea, palpitations, hyperventilation, paresthesia, sweating, flushing, tremor, headache, urinary frequency). Avoid asking about possible medication side effects (i.e., dry mouth, constipation)
0= Absent
1= Mild
2= Moderate
3= Severe
4= Incapacitating

12. SOMATIC SYMPTOMS (GASTROINTESTINAL)
0= None

1= Loss of appetite but eating without encouragement from others. Food intake about normal

2= Difficulty eating without urging from others. Marked reduction of appetite and food intake

13. SOMATIC SYMPTOMS GENERAL
0= None

1= Heaviness in limbs, back or head. Backaches, headache, muscle aches. Loss of energy and fatigability

2= Any clear-cut symptom rates 2

14. GENITAL SYMPTOMS (Symptoms such as: loss of libido; impaired sexual performance; menstrual disturbances)
0= Absent 1= Mild 2= Severe

15. HYPOCHONDRIASIS
0= Not present

1= Self-absorption (bodily)

2= Preoccupation with health

3= Frequent complaints, requests for help, etc. 4= Hypochondriacal delusions

16. LOSS OF WEIGHT
A. When rating by history:

0= No weight loss

1= Probably weight loss associated with present illness 2= Definite (according to patient) weight loss

3= Not assessed

17. INSIGHT
0= Acknowledges being depressed and ill

1= Acknowledges illness but attributes cause to bad food, climate, overwork, virus, need for rest, etc.

2= Denies being ill at all

Total Score

Source: *Journal of Neurology, Neurosurgery and Psychiatry,* 1960: v 23, p 56-61.

appendix i

HISTORY OF VNS AND DEPRESSION

FDA GRANTS EXPEDITED REVIEW STATUS TO CYBERONICS'S NCP SYSTEM for the Treatment of Depression

HOUSTON, July 26, 1999 /PRNewswire/ — Cyberonics, Inc. (Nasdaq: CYBX) today reported that the United States Food and Drug Administration (FDA) granted Expedited Review status for a future Premarket Approval Application for the Cyberonics' NCP System for the treatment of major depressive episodes in patients with unipolar and bipolar depressive disorder. FDA grants Expedited Review status in order to provide for more effective treatment or diagnosis of life-threatening or irreversibly debilitating diseases or conditions. FDA grants Expedited Review status to devices which are intended to treat or diagnose such diseases and conditions, and which typically represent a break-through technology which may provide major (not incremental) increased effectiveness or reduced risk compared to existing, FDA-Approved therapies.

According to recent World Health Organization (www.who.int/inf-fs/en/fact217.html) and other studies, depression is a major public health problem in the United States and worldwide. Depression was the number one cause of disability worldwide in 1990, with 340 million people suffering from major depression. The incident of depressive illness increases with age, and depression is expected to be the second leading cause of disease burden in 2020. In the United States, an estimated 6 million people are being actively treated for depression. Recurrence (multiple episodes) of depression runs as high as 80% of cases. An estimated 1 million people in the United States suffer from treatment resistant chronic depression. An estimated 1 million people worldwide and 100,000 people in the U.S. are treated annually with electroconvulsive therapy (ECT). Depression is a very expensive and life- threatening disorder. Depression costs in the United States are estimated at $40 billion a year in lost work and healthcare costs, $12.4 billion of which are direct treatment costs. A depressed person is 35 times more likely to commit suicide and 15% of chronic depression cases end in suicide.

# #

Cyberonics, Inc. Announces Start of Pivotal Clinical Study of Vagus Nerve Stimulation in Depression

U.S. Food and Drug Administration Approves Final Study Protocol; First Five Clinical Sites Are Initiated with Patient Enrollment Now Underway

HOUSTON, Aug. 2, 2000 /PRNewswire/ — Cyberonics, Inc. (Nasdaq: CYBX) today announced the start of the pivotal clinical study of Vagus Nerve Stimulation (VNS) with the Cyberonics NeuroCybernetic Prosthesis System (NCP(R)) for the treatment of depression. The U.S. Food and Drug Administration (FDA) has approved the final study treatment protocol (D-02) and the first five clinical study sites have been initiated by Cyberonics. The University of Minnesota is the first D-02 Study site to enroll a patient.

Additionally, the University of Miami, Saint Louis University, Medical University of South Carolina in Charleston, and Baylor College of Medicine in Houston have also been initiated and have begun enrolling patients with nine total patients now enrolled. Cyberonics anticipates that the study will include a total of 210 implanted patients at 20 sites. The remaining sites are expected to be initiated by December of 2000, and enrollment in the clinical study is projected to conclude in the summer of 2002. The approved protocol for the D-02 Study calls for a randomized, double-blind, placebo-controlled study with similar inclusion and exclusion criteria used in the depression pilot clinical study. As D-02 study sites are initiated, they will be listed on the Cyberonics Website at www.cyberonics.com/depression. Patients interested in the study may also contact Cyberonics at 888-748-1652 to obtain information about the location of the study sites."

# #

Cyberonics Announces Final Implant in 21-Site, Phase III U.S. Pivotal Study of Vagus Nerve Stimulation for Depression

HOUSTON--(BUSINESS WIRE)--July 11, 2001--Neuro-Cybernetic Prosthesis System Implanted in 235 Patients,
Preliminary Study Results Likely Available by March 2002

Cyberonics, Inc. (Nasdaq:CYBX) today announced that the 235th and final patient received and implant of the NeuroCybernetic Prosthesis (NCP(R)) System as part of the company's expanded U.S. phase III pivotal study of vagus nerve stimulation (VNS) for chronic or recurrent depression. In June 2001, Cyberonics received approval from the United States Food and Drug Administration (FDA) to expand the original study protocol from 210 to up to 240 patients.

Robert P. ("Skip") Cummins, Cyberonics' chairman and chief executive officer, commented, "The FDA approved Cyberonics' request to expand the depression pivotal study in two weeks, and within three weeks of that approval, the final implant occurred. The additional patient experience will strengthen the study and should not result in any delays. The last pivotal study patient should complete the acute phase of the study by the end of October and we remain on track to release the preliminary results of the depression pivotal study by March 2002."

VNS therapy is delivered by the Cyberonics NCP System, an implantable medical device similar to a cardiac pacemaker, which delivers mild electrical stimulation to the left vagus nerve in the patient's neck. Implantation of the stimulation generator and electrode is typically done on an outpatient basis in approximately one hour. Various mechanism of action studies suggest that VNS modulates activity in the areas of the brain responsible for mood, motivation, sleep, appetite and alertness.

# #

FDA Approves Cyberonics' VNS Therapy(TM) System for Treatment-Resistant Depression (TRD) Friday July 15, 4:53 pm ET

HOUSTON, July 15, 2005 /PRNewswire-FirstCall/ — Cyberonics, Inc. (Nasdaq: CYBX - News) today announced that the United States Food and Drug Administration (FDA) approved the Vagus Nerve Stimulation (VNS) Therapy System "for the adjunctive long-term treatment of chronic or recurrent depression for patients 18 years of age or older who are experiencing a major depressive episode and have not had an adequate response to four or more adequate antidepressant treatments."

VNS Therapy is delivered from a small pacemaker-like generator implanted in the chest that sends prepro-grammed, intermittent, mild electrical pulses through the vagus nerve in the neck to the brain. The VNS Therapy System is the first FDA-approved implantable device-based treatment for depression and the first treatment developed, studied, approved and labeled specifically for patients with treatment-resistant depression (TRD).

The VNS Therapy System was approved as a treatment for medically refractory epilepsy in Europe in 1994 and in the United States and Canada in 1997 and as a treatment for TRD in Europe and Canada in 2001. Over 32,000 patients worldwide have accumulated over 94,000 patient years of experience with the VNS Therapy System. The VNS Therapy System is now commercially available for the treatment-resistant depression and refractory epilepsy approved uses in the United States, European Union and Canada. For more information on VNS Therapy for treat-ment-resistant depression, including the contraindications, warnings and precautions, see the Physician's and Patient's Manuals and other information at http://www.cyberonics.com or http://www.vnstherapy.com or call 1-877-NOW 4 VNS.

Major depressive disorder is one of the most prevalent

and serious illnesses in the U.S., affecting nearly 19 million Americans every year. According to the National Institute of Mental Health, depression is the leading cause of disability in the United States and worldwide. Approximately 20 percent of depressed Americans, or approximately four million people, experience chronic or recurrent TRD that has failed to respond to multiple antidepressant treatments including antidepressant medications, talk therapy and in some cases, ECT (electroconvulsive therapy).

"Today for the first time, Americans with treatment-resistant depression have an FDA-approved, informatively-labeled, long-term treatment option for their lifelong and life-threatening illness," commented Robert P. ("Skip") Cummins, Cyberonics' Chairman of the Board and Chief Executive Officer. "The safety and effectiveness of VNS Therapy was demonstrated in up to two-year studies of patients with the most chronic and resistant depressions ever studied. The unprecedented-in-antidepressants product labeling includes all the relevant safety and effectiveness data from the TRD studies and almost 100,000 patient years of epilepsy commercial experience. The TRD labeling will be updated over time by equally unprecedented post-market surveillance, including a 460-patient randomized dosing study and a 2,000-patient, five-year TRD patient registry to facilitate fully-informed VNS treatment decisions by psychiatrists, patients and their families and payers for years to come.

"Seven years ago, Cyberonics, psychiatric thought leaders and a group of courageous Americans with treatment-resistant depression embarked on a seemingly impossible mission to pioneer the first safe and effective treatment for TRD," continued Mr. Cummins. "Today's approval of the first and only treatment developed, studied, approved and labeled specifically for patients with treatment-resistant depression, some 21 months after submission of the Expedited review PMA-Supplement and more than a year after a specially chosen FDA Advisory Panel of Experts recommended approval, is a tribute primarily to (1) over 400 Americans who participated in the VNS studies and made their voices heard during the approval process, (2) psychiatric thought leaders, including Drs. A. John Rush, Harold Sackeim, Mark George and Lauren Marangell, who provided invaluable leadership, guidance and support over the past seven years, (3) the leadership and personnel in FDA's Center for Devices and Radiological Health, Office of Device Evaluation, Office of Surveillance and Biometrics, Office of Compliance, PMA Staff and Dallas District Office whose dedicated public service resulted in approval, and (4) Dr. Richard Rudolph, Vice President of Clinical and Medical Affairs and Chief Medical Officer, Alan Totah, Vice President of Regulatory Affairs and Quality, and the other dedicated men and women of Cyberonics who never waiver from their mission to improve the lives of people touched by chronic, treatment-resistant disorders.

"Today's approval will likely prove to be a transforming event not only for millions of Americans with TRD, but also for Cyberonics, the entire neuromodulation industry and hundreds of thousands of Americans suffering from refractory epilepsy and comorbid TRD," continued Mr. Cummins. "The hundreds of thousands of Americans who suffer from refractory epilepsy and TRD today have their first treatment option approved for each of their primary and most significant, comorbid illnesses. Considering the magnitude of the unmet need in TRD, today's approval will likely firmly establish the brain and neuromodulation as the next frontier for medical devices similar to the heart and cardiac rhythm management in the early sixties. Last but not least, today's approval transforms Cyberonics' mission from improving the lives of approximately one million people worldwide touched by refractory epilepsy to improving the lives of over ten million people worldwide touched by either refractory epilepsy or treatment-resistant depression.

"Cyberonics is much better prepared to accomplish its mission today, than it was in 1997 at the time of epilepsy approval," continued Mr. Cummins. "In 1997 when the VNS Therapy System was first approved by FDA, the device was a new device, the therapy was a revolutionary new therapy and Cyberonics was a new device company with no U.S. commercial experience. Today, the Company, the therapy and the VNS device that was approved as a treatment for TRD have not only survived, but also thrived in eight years of commercial use and in seven years of rigorous TRD studies. VNS is today a proven, safe, effective and cost-effective therapy with good coverage, coding and reimbursement, whose approved use, like so many anti-epileptic drug precedents, is expanding to another indication. The epilepsy and TRD studies and epilepsy commercial experience confirm that VNS offers patients and their families, prescribing physicians, surgeons, hospitals and payers a unique value proposition and benefit to risk ratio that for many is sustained or improves over time. Furthermore, Cyberonics has proven its unwavering commitment to people with chronic, treatment-resistant illnesses through long-term clinical studies, quality products, fully informative labeling, rigorous post-market surveillance to document post-approval safety and effectiveness, and fair and balanced promotion policies and practices. Today, approximately 330 well- trained customer support personnel are beginning to satisfy the very specific needs of patients with TRD, their families, psychiatrists and payers as well as the needs of our existing epilepsy customers. The details of how Cyberonics will go about satisfying those needs, enabling fully-informed VNS treatment decisions, accomplishing its mission of improving the lives of people with chronic, treatment-resistant illnesses and becoming the clear market leader in neuromodulation, the next frontier for medical devices, will be discussed on the conference call scheduled for Monday morning and during the Investor Day at Cyberonics on July 25-26, 2005."

# #

DEPARTMENT OF HEALTH & HUMAN SERVICES   Public Health Service

                                                        Food and Drug Administration
                                                        9200 Corporate Boulevard
                                                        Rockville MD 20850

JUL 1 5 2005

Ms. Annette Zinn, M.P.H., J.D., RAC
Director and Senior Counsel, Regulatory Affairs
Cyberonics, Inc.
100 Cyberonics Boulevard
Houston, TX 77058

Re: P970003/S50
    VNS Therapy System
    Filed: October 27, 2003
    Amended: December 4 and 19, 2003; February 17, March 18 and 29, April 5 and 8, July 7
             and 8, September 8 and 23, 2004; and March 11, and June 28, 2005
    Procode: MUZ

Dear Ms. Zinn:

The Center for Devices and Radiological Health (CDRH) of the Food and Drug Administration
(FDA) has completed its review of your premarket approval application (PMA) supplement for
the VNS Therapy System. This device is indicated for the adjunctive long-term treatment of
chronic or recurrent depression for patients 18 years of age or older who are experiencing a major
depressive episode and have not had an adequate response to four or more adequate
antidepressant treatments. The PMA supplement is approved. You may begin commercial
distribution of the device as modified in accordance with the conditions described below and in
the "Conditions of Approval" (enclosed).

The sale, distribution, and use of this device are restricted to prescription use in accordance with
21 CFR 801.109 within the meaning of section 520(e) of the Federal Food, Drug, and Cosmetic
Act (the act) under the authority of section 515(d)(1)(B)(ii) of the act. FDA has also determined
that, to ensure the safe and effective use of the device, the device is further restricted within the
meaning of section 520(e) under the authority of section 515(d)(1)(B)(ii), (1) insofar as the
labeling specify the requirements that apply to the training of practitioners who may use the
device as approved in this order and (2) insofar as the sale, distribution, and use must not violate
sections 502(q) and (r) of the act.

In addition to the postapproval requirements outlined in the enclosure, you must conduct the
following postapproval studies to further characterize the optimal stimulation dosing and patient
selection criteria for the VNS Therapy System for treatment-resistant depression (TRD). The
first study is a prospective, multicenter, randomized, double-blind comparison of different output
currents in 450 new subjects with TRD. You have agreed to assess the effectiveness responses to
differing outputs 16 weeks after the end of a 4-6 week titration period during which concomitant
therapies will not be changed. You have also agreed to follow these subjects for at least one year
following implantation to further characterize duration of response as well as safety parameters at

Page 2 - Ms. Annette Zinn, M.P.H., J.D., RAC

these higher doses. The second study is a prospective, observation registry study of 1000 implanted subjects with TRD with follow-up extending to 5 years after implantation. This study is designed to evaluate long-term patient outcomes as well as predictors of response to therapy. Post approval study progress reports and results will be submitted as a report to the PMA at 6 month intervals. As appropriate, CDRH may request panel review of the postapproval study data. When necessary, the results will be incorporated into the labeling, via a supplement.

CDRH does not evaluate information related to contract liability warranties, however you should be aware that any such warranty statements must be truthful, accurate, and not misleading, and must be consistent with applicable Federal and State laws.

CDRH will notify the public of its decision to approve your PMA by making available a summary of the safety and effectiveness data upon which the approval is based. The information can be found on the FDA CDRH Internet HomePage located at http://www.fda.gov/cdrh/pmapage.html. Written requests for this information can also be made to the Dockets Management Branch (HFA-305), Food and Drug Administration, 5630 Fishers Lane, rm. 1061, Rockville, MD 20852. The written request should include the PMA number or docket number. Within 30 days from the date that this information is placed on the Internet, any interested person may seek review of this decision by requesting an opportunity for administrative review, either through a hearing or review by an independent advisory committee under section 515(g) of the Federal Food, Drug, and Cosmetic Act (the act).

Failure to comply with any postapproval requirement constitutes a ground for withdrawal of approval of a PMA. Commercial distribution of a device that is not in compliance with these conditions is a violation of the act.

You are reminded that, as soon as possible and before commercial distribution of your device, you must submit an amendment to this PMA submission with copies of all approved labeling affected by this supplement in final printed form. The labeling will not routinely be reviewed by FDA staff when PMA supplement applicants include with their submission of the final printed labeling a cover letter stating that the final printed labeling is identical to the labeling approved i draft form. If the final printed labeling is not identical, any changes from the final draft labeling should be highlighted and explained in the amendment.

All required documents should be submitted in triplicate, unless otherwise specified, to the address below and should reference the above PMA number to facilitate processing.

> PMA Document Mail Center (HFZ-401)
> Center for Devices and Radiological Health
> Food and Drug Administration
> 9200 Corporate Blvd.
> Rockville, Maryland 20850

Page 3 - Ms. Annette Zinn, M.P.H., J.D., RAC

If you have any questions concerning this approval order, please contact me at (301) 827-7975.

Sincerely yours,

Daniel Schultz, M.D.
Director
Center for Devices and
   Radiological Health
Food and Drug Administration

Enclosure

Last Modified: 1-31-02

CONDITIONS OF APPROVAL

<u>PREMARKET APPROVAL APPLICATION (PMA) SUPPLEMENT</u>. Before making any change affecting the safety or effectiveness of the device, submit a PMA supplement for review and approval by FDA unless the change is of a type for which a "Special PMA Supplement-Changes Being Effected" is permitted under 21 CFR 814.39(d) or an alternate submission is permitted in accordance with 21 CFR 814.39(e) or (f). A PMA supplement or alternate submission shall comply with applicable requirements under 21 CFR 814.39 of the final rule for Premarket Approval of Medical Devices.

All situations that require a PMA supplement cannot be briefly summarized; therefore, please consult the PMA regulation for further guidance. The guidance provided below is only for several key instances.

A PMA supplement must be submitted when unanticipated adverse effects, increases in the incidence of anticipated adverse effects, or device failures necessitate a labeling, manufacturing, or device modification.

A PMA supplement must be submitted if the device is to be modified and the modified device should be subjected to animal or laboratory or clinical testing designed to determine if the modified device remains safe and effective.

A "<u>Special PMA Supplement - Changes Being Effected</u>" is limited to the labeling, quality control and manufacturing process changes specified under 21 CFR 814.39(d)(2). It allows for the addition of, but not the replacement of previously approved, quality control specifications and test methods. These changes may be implemented before FDA approval upon acknowledgment by FDA that the submission is being processed as a "Special PMA Supplement - Changes Being Effected." This procedure is not applicable to changes in device design, composition, specifications, circuitry, software or energy source.

<u>Alternate submissions</u> permitted under 21 CFR 814.39(e) apply to changes that otherwise require approval of a PMA supplement before implementation of the change and include the use of a <u>30-day PMA supplement</u> or <u>annual postapproval report (see below)</u>. FDA must have previously indicated in an advisory opinion to the affected industry or in correspondence with the applicant that the alternate submission is permitted for the change. Before such can occur, FDA and the PMA applicant(s) involved must agree upon any needed testing protocol, test results, reporting format, information to be reported, and the alternate submission to be used.

<u>Alternate submissions</u> permitted under 21 CFR 814.39(f) for manufacturing process changes include the use of a 30-day Notice. The manufacturer may distribute the device 30 days after the date on which the FDA receives the 30-day Notice, unless the FDA notifies the applicant within 30 days from receipt of the notice that the notice is not adequate.

POSTAPPROVAL REPORTS. Continued approval of this PMA is contingent upon the submission of postapproval reports required under 21 CFR 814.84 at intervals of 1 year from the date of approval of the original PMA. Postapproval reports for supplements approved under the original PMA, if applicable, are to be included in the next and subsequent annual reports for the original PMA unless specified otherwise in the approval order for the PMA supplement. Two copies identified as "Annual Report" and bearing the applicable PMA reference number are to be submitted to the PMA Document Mail Center (HFZ-401), Center for Devices and Radiological Health, Food and Drug Administration, 9200 Corporate Blvd., Rockville, Maryland 20850. The postapproval report shall indicate the beginning and ending date of the period covered by the report and shall include the following information required by 21 CFR 814.84:

1.   Identification of changes described in 21 CFR 814.39(a) and changes required to be reported to FDA under 21 CFR 814.39(b).

2.   Bibliography and summary of the following information not previously submitted as part of the PMA and that is known to or reasonably should be known to the applicant:

   a. unpublished reports of data from any clinical investigations or nonclinical laboratory studies involving the device or related devices ("related" devices include devices which are the same or substantially similar to the applicant's device); and

   b. reports in the scientific literature concerning the device.

If, after reviewing the bibliography and summary, FDA concludes that agency review of one or more of the above reports is required, the applicant shall submit two copies of each identified report when so notified by FDA.

ADVERSE REACTION AND DEVICE DEFECT REPORTING. As provided by 21 CFR 814.82(a)(9), FDA has determined that in order to provide continued reasonable assurance of the safety and effectiveness of the device, the applicant shall submit 3 copies of a written report identified, as applicable, as an "Adverse Reaction Report" or "Device Defect Report" to the PMA Document Mail Center (HFZ-401), Center for Devices and Radiological Health, Food and Drug Administration, 9200 Corporate Blvd., Rockville, Maryland 20850 within 10 days after the applicant receives or has knowledge of information concerning:

1.   A mix-up of the device or its labeling with another article.

2.   Any adverse reaction, side effect, injury, toxicity, or sensitivity reaction that is attributable to the device and:

   a. has not been addressed by the device's labeling; or

   b. has been addressed by the device's labeling but is occurring with unexpected severity or frequency.

3. Any significant chemical, physical or other change or deterioration in the device, or any failure of the device to meet the specifications established in the approved PMA that could not cause or contribute to death or serious injury but are not correctable by adjustments or other maintenance procedures described in the approved labeling. The report shall include a discussion of the applicant's assessment of the change, deterioration or failure and any proposed or implemented corrective action by the applicant. When such events are correctable by adjustments or other maintenance procedures described in the approved labeling, all such events known to the applicant shall be included in the Annual Report described under "Postapproval Reports" above unless specified otherwise in the conditions of approval to this PMA. This postapproval report shall appropriately categorize these events and include the number of reported and otherwise known instances of each category during the reporting period. Additional information regarding the events discussed above shall be submitted by the applicant when determined by FDA to be necessary to provide continued reasonable assurance of the safety and effectiveness of the device for its intended use.

REPORTING UNDER THE MEDICAL DEVICE REPORTING (MDR) REGULATION.

The Medical Device Reporting (MDR) Regulation became effective on December 13, 1984. This regulation was replaced by the reporting requirements of the Safe Medical Devices Act of 1990 which became effective July 31, 1996 and requires that all manufacturers and importers of medical devices, including in vitro diagnostic devices, report to the FDA whenever they receive or otherwise become aware of information, from any source, that reasonably suggests that a device marketed by the manufacturer or importer:

1. May have caused or contributed to a death or serious injury; or

2. Has malfunctioned and such device or similar device marketed by the manufacturer or importer would be likely to cause or contribute to a death or serious injury if the malfunction were to recur.

The same events subject to reporting under the MDR Regulation may also be subject to the above "Adverse Reaction and Device Defect Reporting" requirements in the "Conditions of Approval" for this PMA. FDA has determined that such duplicative reporting is unnecessary. Whenever an event involving a device is subject to reporting under both the MDR Regulation and the "Conditions of Approval" for a PMA, the manufacturer shall submit the appropriate reports required by the MDR Regulation within the time frames as identified in 21 CFR 803.10(c) using FDA Form 3500A, i.e., 30 days after becoming aware of a reportable death, serious injury, or malfunction as described in 21 CFR 803.50 and 21 CFR 803.52 and 5 days after becoming aware that a reportable MDR event requires remedial action to prevent an unreasonable risk of substantial harm to the public health. The manufacturer is responsible for submitting a baseline report on FDA Form 3417 for a device when the device model is first reported under 21 CFR 803.50. This baseline report is to include the PMA reference number. Any written report and its envelope is to be specifically identified, e.g., "Manufacturer Report," "5-Day Report," "Baseline Report," etc.

Any written report is to be submitted to:

Food and Drug Administration
Center for Devices and Radiological Health
Medical Device Reporting
PO Box 3002
Rockville, Maryland 20847-3002

Copies of the MDR Regulation (FOD # 336&1336)and FDA publications entitled "An Overvie
of the Medical Device Reporting Regulation" (FOD # 509) and "Medical Device Reporting for
Manufacturers" (FOD #987) are available on the CDRH WWW Home Page. They are also
available through CDRH's Fact-On-Demand (F-O-D) at 800-899-0381. Written requests for
information can be made by sending a facsimile to CDRH's Division of Small Manufacturers
International and Consumer Assistance (DSMICA) at 301-443-8818.

INDEX

213

*For more information on VNS Therapy for the
treatment of chronic depression,
and to order copies of this book,
please visit our Website:*

www.VagusNerveStimulator.com